"If you are looking to bring more ritual and magic into your life, you will love this book! *Positive Pagan* reawakens our connection with nature and the art of ritual work, helping us to create a more meaningful, aligned, and positive life. An inspiring read for anyone searching to create a richer and more harmonious connection with the world."

—Tanaaz Chubb, author of *The Power of Positive Energy*

"Don't be fooled: *Positive Pagan* is not a fluffy book full of 'just be happy' spiritual bypassing! This is real, magical, brave, full-spectrum living. So if you want to be positive, but you know denying or covering your negative feelings just isn't going to cut it, this book is for you. It will help you live your best and most joyful life."

—Tess Whitehurst, author of *The Self-Love Superpower*

"Equally wise and comforting, Lisa Wagoner offers excellent tools, tips, and rituals all for the benefit of the practitioner, wherever they may be on their path. This book should be go-to reading for anyone who desires to wield their personal power for the good of themselves and their communities."

—Lauren Devora, author of the Children of Lilith series

"From creating simple altars to healthy use of social media, Lisa Wagoner offers us her wisdom for walking an optimistic path. *Positive Pagan* is a fabulous resource of ideas, exercises, and rituals gently guiding the reader to the sunnier side of earth-based spirituality. This book is a wonderful antidote to the infectious negativity that is the true plague of our times."

—Cyndi Brannen, PhD, author of
Keeping Her Keys* and *Entering Hekate's Garden

POSITIVE
PAGAN

© Kimfluence Photography

About the Author

Lisa Wagoner is a Patheos Pagan blogger (*Witch, Indeed*) and the Maven of Mystical Curation at the Of Wand & Earth metaphysical shop. She has presented workshops at Mystic South, Sacred Space Conference, and the Rota Psychic Expos, is an ordained Pagan priestess and minister, and is a certified Reiki Master in both Usui and Celtic traditions. In addition to her cohosting duties at the podcast *Mystic Tea*, she has also contributed to the anthologies *The Witch's Altar*, *My Wandering Uterus*, and *Queens of the Quill*. Visit her online at www.LisaWagoner.com.

Staying Upbeat in an Offbeat World

POSITIVE

PAGAN

LISA WAGONER

Llewellyn Publications
Woodbury, Minnesota

FIRST EDITION
First Printing, 2022

Book design by Valerie A. King
Cover design by Shannon McKuhen
Editing by Rhiannon Nelson

Llewellyn Publications is a registered trademark of Llewellyn Worldwide Ltd.

Library of Congress Cataloging-in-Publication Data
Names: Wagoner, Lisa, author.
Title: Positive pagan : staying upbeat in an offbeat world / Lisa Wagoner.
Description: First edition. | Woodbury, Minnesota : Llewellyn Publications,
    2022. | Includes bibliographical references.
Identifiers: LCCN 2022001911 (print) | LCCN 2022001912 (ebook) | ISBN
    9780738765341 (paperback) | ISBN 9780738765518 (ebook)
Subjects: LCSH: Optimism—Miscellanea. | Magic. | Witches. | Neopagans.
Classification: LCC BF1621 .W335 2022 (print) | LCC BF1621 (ebook) | DDC
    133.4/3—dc23/eng/20220322
LC record available at https://lccn.loc.gov/2022001911
LC ebook record available at https://lccn.loc.gov/2022001912

Llewellyn Worldwide Ltd. does not participate in, endorse, or have any authority or responsibility concerning private business transactions between our authors and the public.

All mail addressed to the author is forwarded but the publisher cannot, unless specifically instructed by the author, give out an address or phone number.

Any internet references contained in this work are current at publication time, but the publisher cannot guarantee that a specific location will continue to be maintained. Please refer to the publisher's website for links to authors' websites and other sources.

Llewellyn Publications
A Division of Llewellyn Worldwide Ltd.
2143 Wooddale Drive
Woodbury, MN 55125-2989
www.llewellyn.com

Printed in the United States of America

For Elliot and Evan, my beloved and wonderful sons.
Thank you for teaching me so much.

Disclaimer

The publisher and the author assume no liability for any injuries caused to the reader that may result from the reader's use of content contained in this publication and recommend common sense when contemplating the practices described in the work.

CONTENTS

Acknowledgments

To Trevor, all my love and gratitude. Thank you for your love,
inspiration, encouragement, and support.
I can't wait to see what's next.

To my Oma and Mom, for nurturing and challenging me.
I miss you both always.

To Nicole Czysz, Lauren Devora, Oreon Millard, and Veronica
Stephens, for being my support and sounding boards.
You kept me going so many times, thank you so much.

To Heather Greene and Rhiannon Nelson, with thanks for your
editing and word magic.

To Jason Mankey at Patheos Pagan, thank you for setting me on the
path of blogging at Patheos, and for your support and guidance.

To Pascha Haninah, for being a guiding light and mentor
in so many ways.

To Patti Wigington, for writing the foreword to this book. With
many thanks for all the joy and excitement you bring to my life.

To Andrew Hozier-Byrne, with heartfelt gratitude for your music
and inspiring words. They were the background during the writing
of this book. Indeed, we are the Pagans of the good times.

To all those who enjoyed my writing through the years, and took
the time to tell me so. I appreciated every single one.

To my community, far-flung and near, worldwide and local,
thank you. You are in my heart.

I wrote this book in honor of the goddess Brigid, who has guided
and shown me so much. I remain grateful.

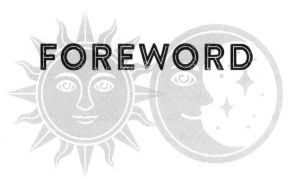

FOREWORD

There's an old adage that positive thinking is the key to success, but for most people, staying positive when the world is falling apart can be a real struggle. How in the world are you supposed to "think positive" when you're stressed out over work, your family has issues, you're dealing with financial problems, and on top of all that, there's a global pandemic raging?

It ain't easy.

And yet, positivity can lead to a groundbreaking, life-changing shift in your mindset. It's not about sunshine and rainbows and unicorns 24/7, although that wouldn't necessarily be a bad thing—who doesn't like sunshine and rainbows and unicorns? Instead, it's about reevaluating your life in a way that allows you to look for the good—however small or fleeting it may be—and celebrating it when you identify it. Positivity is about making a choice to not let the insignificant things get you down when you know in the grand scheme of things, they just don't matter that much. We can't control many things around us, including other people, but we can control how we respond to them.

Someone once said to me, "You always seem just so darn happy." To this day, I still don't know if it was a thinly veiled insult or not, but regardless, I found it odd, because just like everyone else, I have my down days. I have mornings where there isn't enough coffee in the world to make my day not stink. I get frustrated and annoyed at things I can't change and at people who inconvenience others. There have been moments where I was just one broken shoelace away from a full-on meltdown.

Nevertheless, I persist. Because I realized a long time ago that no matter how Pollyanna-ish it might seem, I could try to find the good in any circumstance. I might not succeed in finding it, sure … but it was the *trying* that mattered.

I've been practicing as a witch and Pagan for more than three decades, well over half my time on earth. And for some of those early years, I did all the things I thought real witches were supposed to do. I cast circles, I curated a nice little collection of herbs and crystals and candles, I diligently marked moon phases on my calendar…but I wasn't satisfied. For a while, I wondered if maybe the problem was the magic itself—maybe it wasn't real after all!— but I knew other people who were practicing and who had successful and happy lives.

Then I started to doubt my own abilities—perhaps the magic was real, but I just sucked at it. That was certainly a possibility … but then, over time, I came to a surprising (and somewhat alarming) epiphany. When things were good for me—mentally, physically, emotionally—my magic was successful. On the other hand, when my mundane life was hitting a rough patch … well. So did my magic.

Was it possible that my magic was directly influenced by my own thought process? Could I have been unconsciously self-sabotaging by expecting things to fail?

That was a hard truth for me. Full stop, it forced me to reevaluate everything I was doing, feeling, thinking … and believing. And so, being a logically minded person, I decided to test the theory. I chose to deliberately see positive aspects of a situation, even when it felt like everything was negative. At work, I was called into my supervisor's office and coached on ways I could improve; rather than see this as an abject failure of my own professional abilities, I instead told myself this was an *opportunity*, a moment for learning and improving. When my first marriage began to crumble, I tried to look past the financial hardship and emotional turmoil that would result from suddenly becoming the single parent of a toddler—rather, this was a chance to reinvent myself and build my life from scratch, facing and overcoming obstacles and challenges to make a better life for my child.

You know what happened? Things got *better*. Not just in my mundane life, but my magical and spiritual one as well. By finding the positive—however faint that glimmer of hope might be—I refocused my mindset, reclaiming my own power, and my magical practice followed suit.

From there, my sense of contentment and satisfaction grew exponentially. Sure, there were times that were hard—anyone who's ever been a single parent with a minimal income knows that story—but overall, I learned to find happiness. I came to understand how to be satisfied with the things I had, and that working toward achieving new goals was a positive growth challenge to be celebrated, not feared or avoided. Perhaps equally important, I discovered the value of gratitude, something I still rejoice in today, thirty-odd years later—because the more I have to be thankful for, the more I tend to attract additional things that bring me joy. Over time, I taught myself to cultivate a life full of positive, loving, kind people—and when I feel positive, loving, and kind myself, I share it with others, and the circle builds and expands.

You always seem just so darn happy. It felt like an accusation of sorts when it was said, almost as if *how dare you be this upbeat*, as though I had no right to be. But I do—I've earned it—and more important, I make a choice each day. I decide, consciously and with full awareness, that I can either see the glass as half empty or as half full. Things can be a struggle or an opportunity, and how I tackle them head-on will directly influence the outcome.

The same is true of magic. If we view magic as a way to change that which dissatisfies us, why wouldn't we face it with a positive mindset? Think about how many times you've begun a spell or ritual, and paused for a moment, thinking *I don't think this is gonna work*. You probably plodded ahead anyway… and the results were less than stellar, confirming those initial doubts. But what if, rather than questioning the efficacy of the working, you simply threw yourself into it, thinking *This is going to work and it will be amazing*. How would that change the endgame?

I once read a quote that said something like *Whether you believe you will succeed or you believe you will fail, you're right*. Envision the power your magic could have if you believe—truly, in your heart and soul—that every single working was going to be a success.

Shifting your mindset to a positive one isn't an immediate process. It's a lifelong journey, and I guarantee you'll hit bumps in the road. However, it genuinely is a conscious choice. You'll have to learn to prioritize your own needs—I know, that's hard!—and show yourself the same courtesy and grace you offer to those you love. You might discover it's time to cut ties with people who bring you down rather than lift you up—also hard, because when someone's been around a long time it's tough to end a relationship. Perhaps the most difficult part will be, after years of seeing the negative aspects of every situation, convincing yourself that you really are going to be okay.

I've known Lisa Wagoner for many years, and when she told me she was writing a book called *Positive Pagan*, I was so excited— because, frankly, I couldn't think of a better person to write such a thing. In the time Lisa and I have been friends, I've seen her face numerous battles—those stories aren't mine to share, but she'll get into them in more depth shortly—but somehow, despite it all, she keeps climbing upward. No matter what life throws at her, she stays resilient and upbeat and manages to find joy and reverence in the midst of struggles that would have beaten so many people down.

In the coming chapters, Lisa shares her tips on not just living in a positive way as a Pagan, but also how to shift your mindset. You'll learn the value of finding the sacred and creating a magical space, working with nature, and the importance of community in all its many forms. By the time you reach the end, I truly believe you'll have a deeper, richer understanding of not just *why* positivity matters, but how you can use it to bring about change for the better in your own life—spiritually, physically, and emotionally.

As I mentioned, creating and cultivating a positive mindset is a lifelong journey—but you can do it. You can take a stand, make a mark, and bring joy and contentment into your own life. When you develop this new mindset, you can choose to manifest all the things you want and need. And when you empower yourself this way, you will be unstoppable.

~Patti Wigington
Author of *Herb Magic*, *Witchcraft for Healing*,
and *Badass Ancestors*

INTRODUCTION

Hello, Positive Pagan! As you hold this book in your hands, glancing through the pages, my deepest hope is that you feel elated you found a book on being a Positive Pagan because being generally positive and a Pagan resonates with you. Or perhaps you have a yen to incorporate more positivity into your Paganism and want some ideas and inspiration. Maybe you feel a bit alone in the world of Paganism because positivity doesn't seem that, well … positive—or something you can easily talk about, because the world seems mostly negative. You may even be asking yourself at this point: What exactly is a Positive Pagan?

Pagan as a noun refers to a person who holds beliefs outside of the world's main religions. The usage of the word "Pagan" in this book is a very broad term that encompasses a wide range of people that fall under that umbrella: witches, druids, earth-based religion followers, polytheistic, agnostics, doubters, and the like. There are as many types of Pagans as there are stars in the sky, so all are welcome here as you explore being a Positive Pagan. My focus is more on what is under the broad umbrella of Paganism, without restrictions or gatekeeping. I like to see the connectivity in all things, so the thread of positivity that can and hopefully does run through many of us connects us to the term "Positive Pagan."

I hope this book speaks to many, and I would also note that I don't want the word Pagan to hold you back. Whatever your beliefs—religious, spiritual, or otherwise—I include anyone as Pagan who has stood in awe of nature's beauty. Seems simple enough, right? To me, that is the most distilled core of Paganism, this love and appreciation of nature, no matter what your local geography looks like, and where you live. I'm not interested in labels, gatekeeping, or exclusion, so I prefer the umbrella of Paganism to include all those who feel a pull toward Paganism, are Pagan-curious, or identify as a Pagan in your own unique way.

So, does any of this sound like you? Then read on, my friend. If it doesn't, and you remain curious, please read on as well. All are welcome here!

When used in this book, the term "positive" describes the energy that flows within one's self. No matter the obstacles or hardships, or how wonky or horrific the world seems, positivity helps to move forward. It can be a challenge to stay upbeat in an offbeat world. We are assaulted daily with the negative and terrible news of the world. Yet something within you, like an ember or spark, guides you forward as you navigate the journey called life.

Many of the activities and concepts included in this book focus on action and moving energy toward a specific intent. So if you are exploring Paganism, or you have read or heard about Pagans, or maybe the word positive just caught your eye, consider this a safe space within this book. Whatever your spiritual practice is, these activities are non-denominational and open to all, and my hope is that these rituals and ideas add resonance to your practices.

A long time ago, one of the guides in my life told me that he was impressed that I had the innate ability to find "diamonds in the muck." That has remained my favorite description of the positivity that resonates within not just me, but also within the many people I have met who share this same outlook. To take hardships or challenging times and find something good despite all the muck that surrounds that darkness is not an easy feat. I liken it to a deep feeling of cozy warmth, or a smooth, flowing stream that keeps a person moving onward throughout their life, despite obstacles, life events, and negativity in the world.

It's the deep, inner knowing of the beauty in a sunrise or sunset despite endless gloomy reports on the news. It's self-care, knowing that it remains a priority to keep oneself strong and steady to get through daily life. It's the boundaries that are set, both physically and spiritually, to preserve personal energy. It's the magical practice and spirituality that sustains a person in so many little ways: stirring your coffee a magical number of times, spending consistent time at your altar, or helping a friend who needs a magical boost. It's being out in nature when life feels overwhelming and finding the grounding and centering you need there. It is waking up with gratitude, looking out for others, and a determination to guide your life, aided by spellwork and intention setting.

Being a Positive Pagan can sometimes feel out of step with the rest of the world. Positivity is often equated with being unworldly, naive, or not very intelligent. It may feel like being in the minority around friends, family, or your magical community. Perhaps there is an exasperation when someone focuses on the negative aspects of life, with no appreciation of anything positive or uplifting. Or sometimes it may feel as if positivity needs to be hidden from others, because it might be mocked, laughed at, or ignored.

Many share this feeling, and it's understandable why people tend to keep quiet about their positivity. It may seem like most people around you don't share this positive outlook. There may be many times that we feel the need to keep to ourselves, but in my experience, everyone at some point, no matter how fleeting, feels a bit of that sunshine we seem to access so readily. Positive Pagans tend to guard that bit of sunshine like a precious jewel, but I like to think of its rays radiating outward to other people and the world. It's a gift to be able to do so, and to share this outlook with others, and results in happiness when we find like-minded people who resonate with positivity.

Positive Paganism is also a lifestyle, a series of choices, and a way that your sense of self remains optimistic, despite what's going on in the world or in your personal life. It's a thread that runs throughout your day, from your morning routines, to how you interact with the outside world, the people at work, and with your friends, family, and community. It's the choices that are made, from what you eat, wear, and purchase, to the rituals and celebrations that are part of our lives.

For those of you who may have picked up this book in hopes of experiencing more positivity in your daily life and magical practices: thank you! You may be challenged with feeling positive at all in your present moment, with your life circumstances, mindset, or world events. As a result, your magical practices may have fallen by the wayside. I wrote this book for you as well. It is a universal experience, those times we get offtrack and everything in the world seems the polar opposite of positivity. This is a book you can put down and pick up when needed, for a little boost to get you back on track to being your grounded, positive, centered self.

Before we begin, a few caveats: please know that Positive Paganism and this book is not to be confused with toxic positivity. There won't be any advice or exhortations to remain endlessly positive, or insistence that "just be positive and all will be okay!" Going through life is a constant balancing act, so balance is definitely key in remaining positive. It is the balance of negativity, whether we experience it ourselves, or see it out in the world. A sense of positivity can seem astounding or confusing to those who don't share our outlook.

Positive Paganism isn't about ignoring the existence of a problem or minimizing weighty issues such as racism, nor does it invalidate someone's struggle or pain. Positive Paganism embraces the acknowledgement of problems, pain, and struggle, while advocating for tenacity, perspective, and balance. Utilizing Pagan practices adds a layer of possibility to positive actions toward goals of a fulfilling reality and balance in this sometimes tumultuous, negative world. Positive Paganism doesn't exist in a static void. It is re-engaged regularly and often. Through ritual and suggestions, this book will guide you along that process of discovering and tapping into that positivity. While I firmly believe that positivity resides in all of us, it does take a bit of work to tap into it if you are unfamiliar with accessing that light.

The rituals and concepts that I have included are those that have worked for me. During the time of COVID-19, I myself experienced many months of dark times, dealing with ancestral trauma, revisitations of childhood emotional damage, along with feelings of unworthiness and failure. As I worked my way through this book during the editing process, revisiting the rituals and ideas in this book helped me move through what I was experiencing. It is my hope that they do the same for you.

While I hope this book helps you with your journey, it is by no means a "Do this my way and my way only!" kind of book. There is more than one way to do things, so if you feel something needs to be added, deleted, or tweaked to the practices I discuss, do so. I would like you to consider this a guide and a springboard into creating, building, and supplementing your own lifestyle and rituals.

In addition, this book is also not an instructional guide to magic or witchcraft. Inherent in the word "Paganism" is the belief in other deities, the practice of magic (no matter if you consider yourself a beginner), and a basic knowledge of magic and witchcraft practices. I will provide explanations of the tools and items needed, but none of this will be useful to you without your own personal intention and energy. Intention is the engine of moving energy toward your desired result. So if it is your desire to be a Positive Pagan, set your intention and be sure to add that "extra ingredient" to the spells and practices in this book.

I will often ask you to trust your intuition and inner voice. If you're not sure how to access that, or if you feel it hasn't worked for you before, no problem! I will share a few of my methods to help with this process. Being a Positive Pagan is a journey of learning how to be comfortable with one's self and one's processes, while being authentic and grateful. This journey won't be accomplished in a quick trip, so please be kind to yourself if you feel you're not succeeding.

You may also notice that I embrace the theme of duality throughout this book. I believe that duality is inherent in being a Positive Pagan. Without darkness, there is not an appreciation of light. Being positive understands there are moments of darkness, and that being positive isn't the light at the end of the tunnel. Instead, it is a foundation you build that bubbles up when needed. It's the steady hum or background noise in which we live our lives, and it gives us an inner strength to keep going. We can balance both positive and negative in our lives, just as we can embrace both the light and the darkness. Have you ever had that moment of being happy and sad at the same time? It feels a bit like that.

As you work your way through this book, you may notice a bit of resistance to things that may be unfamiliar. Please don't dismiss it. Instead, acknowledge that resistance and see where that takes you. Sometimes resistance to change can hinder progress or stop you in your tracks. Yet sometimes that is necessary, so we start by simply noticing that resistance and work our way through it. In leaning into Positive Paganism, you will learn to trust that inner voice to find out if something is truly not for you, or if you are resisting a positive change.

One of the foundations of being a Positive Pagan is also this basic principle: it's not all or nothing. The purpose of this book is not to convey that this way is the *only* way; it's just *one* way. A beautiful, multi-layered, full of possibilities, action-oriented kind of way. Being a Positive Pagan is not just an outlook; it's also action and movement. It is making things happen, working on yourself, working with others, and helping the community when you can. It doesn't matter if you are a solitary practitioner or part of a coven or large group. This is a book to pick up when you feel overwhelmed by the negativity, and for those times when you wake up feeling happy and everyone around you is full of gloom and doom. It's a book to refer to when you want to use your magical intentions for positive changes in your life, your community, and the world. There is a time for banework and banishing, and that can be part of being a Positive Pagan as well. As you progress in your journey, it will become easier to balance.

Another facet of being a Positive Pagan is a commitment to living a magical life, winding all the tenets of your life with a thread of magic, intention, and sacred space. As already mentioned, action is key, as the "doing" of things ultimately makes you feel better and propels you forward. Doing things intentionally helps even more.

If we all make positive changes and exude Positive Paganism, how wonderful would that be? Think of all of us in the community, working our own Positive Pagan magic, and the outward rippling effects we could have on the world!

At this point you might be wondering: how did this book come about? I write a regular online blog on the Patheos website called *Witch, Indeed.* A few times a month, I write about all my adventures in my witch life, including my practices, rituals I enjoy, and things that I have learned on my journey. One entry I wrote was called "Being a Positive Pagan in a Dark World." The response was astounding. It resonated with so many people, and I still get messages about that particular entry to this day. It felt as if I touched a nerve, so I looked for books on being a Positive Pagan and didn't really find many on the subject. I began receiving messages via certain events and life reminders that perhaps my daily practices as a Positive Pagan might be useful to others. So, I began to jot down notes of how I live my life as a Positive Pagan. It soon added up to a collection of rituals, concepts, and practices that you now hold in your hand.

How did I personally arrive at embracing Positive Paganism? It began in my childhood, being the youngest of four children, living a somewhat eccentric, bohemian life within a strong matriarchal household. I was raised by my German mom and Austrian grandmother, two opposite ends of the spectrum as far as life philosophies go. Both had survived World War II in Berlin, and its effects on their personalities were completely and utterly different. My mom was an atheist, and had a firm, no-nonsense outlook on life, coupled with what I now believe was untreated trauma from surviving a childhood and young adulthood in a war-torn country. She felt her hopes and dreams had all been dashed by the war and her wartime marriage, and she wanted something different for her children. Her methods were to insist on blunt truths, no matter how hurtful, and a focus on the negatives in life, all of which she used in conjunction with her pessimistic outlook on life to reinforce her ideas. We were strongly encouraged, for example, to read mostly nonfiction so we wouldn't have any dreamy or unrealistic outlooks on life, and thus be caught unawares when life would surely turn out poorly. This was challenging for me because I loved to read all types of books, and I recognized my resistance to my mom's ideas from a very young age. It never made sense to me, even though I couldn't really articulate my resistance. I noticed early on that the more negative outlook she expressed, the more negative things happened to her. Even as a child, I knew these types of ideas were not the kind I wanted to have. I tucked away my thoughts on this, keeping them to myself until I was older.

I have the utmost gratitude for my grandmother, who helped raise me. Although she too had a very realistic outlook on life, she had a friendly, pleasant personality, and she encouraged the reading of fairy tales while teaching me some life truths and folk magic along the way. My Austrian grandmother was outwardly a very sweet and quiet woman, but growing up I realized that she had a steely determination to make the best of whatever situation she found herself in. She always found a way to be grateful, despite some of the horrific life circumstances she had experienced. Remember the guide who told me I could find diamonds in the muck? I fully attribute that to my grandmother and am ever grateful for the lessons I learned from her.

Growing up in an Austrian/German household, my family practiced a bit of folk magic that didn't have specific magical language or words to describe it; it seemed more like family traditions. I absorbed it all, adding my own as I grew up.

We had kitchen witches (a witch figure that hung in the kitchen to ensure good luck and good meals), used manifestation practices (writing down lists of what we wanted to accomplish, and following it up with actions to make things happen), and followed a few folklore adages. When my grandmother hiccupped, she would always say, "Someone is thinking about me!" and sure enough, someone would soon call or come by. Little moments like that were tucked away in my observations, coupled with my desire to be a witch from a young age when I first discovered them in books. I can still see the illustration in my mind's eye of the book when I first encountered witches. I knew then that was something I wanted to be part of my life. Witches made things happen, and since my life was dominated by women (my mom, sisters, and grandmother), in my mind, witches equated power and independence.

My childhood was full of dysfunction, and I approached adulthood with a firm determination to end family and generational patterns.

Life for me then had its own darkness, filled with challenging times, including marriage, divorce, living with others' mental disorders, life-threatening illnesses, severe mental defeat, and suicides by those I loved. Through it all, a steady drumbeat of positivity kept me going. A mixture of both my mom's relentless reality, tempered with my grandmother's hopefulness, resulted in me knowing that despite some extremely dark times in my life, good things were still a possibility.

For many years, I neglected my magical practices in the busyness of life, but I returned to them when I reached a point in my life that I wanted to change my circumstances. Once I started practicing what I had absorbed during my childhood, built on what I had learned since then and evolved in my own practices, I thrived. I felt that trickle of positivity turn into a surge and noticed how circumstances in my life changed for the better.

More and more, ritual and practice were the core of my actions. I began to follow lunar cycles and the Wheel of the Year more closely, using their power to manifest and make things happen. I embarked on different career paths (which I previously didn't think were possible), moved to an area more in tune with my spiritual practices, became a professional writer, was ordained, and began deeper and more meaningful relationships. I could have easily gone down darker and different roads in life, succumbing to the addictions that were prevalent in my family history. There were a few points in time when I could have ended up homeless and alone. Looking back, I know it was my spiritual practices and that core of being a Positive Pagan that kept me course-correcting and on this path that I am now happily on. It is my hope this book will provide inspiration and encouragement on your own journey.

I firmly believe in this way of life and am delighted to share all the knowledge I have gathered throughout my life journey. Consider this a guidebook, a how-to, and a reassurance that you're not alone. It can be a safety valve, a boost, and more. It is for you to use, read, ruminate on, discuss, and create your own practices. A quick magic practice to begin: place bookmarks of bay leaves in the pages you'd like to return to, both as a placeholder and also as an herb of manifestation and prosperity!

I also hope you will consider this book a tool in your Positive Pagan tool kit. I believe that we each have our own tool kit of ways in which we have survived, thrived, and retained our positive spirit. It may consist of habits formed, mantras or sayings that we utilize, or actions taken to keep the positive spirit going within us. Maybe it's a collection of favorite crystals, or following the moon's power, or the Wheel of the Year that keeps you on track. I would be very honored if this book was added to your personal tool kit as well.

First Steps: Fundamentals of Magic for Staying Positive

The first steps in any lifestyle change or addition can be exciting, yet also a little fearful: What is needed? Are specific things required? How do I begin? Is there a lot of work involved? Is it even possible? Good news! The Positive Pagan journey can start anytime you choose, and it is a journey you can return to when needed in your life. Think of it like a suitcase, packed and ready to go on your next trip, but with some room for a few items to add here and there for your journey as needed.

The first steps in this journey include doing some internal work. It involves diving deep into what you want, what you'd like to create, and what you want your life to look like. As in any sort of lifestyle change, it may take some time to incorporate these actions into your day-to-day life until it becomes a habit. Results will not necessarily emerge right away.

The end results, in my opinion, are well worth the effort. It's living your life in harmony with your surroundings. It's incorporating your magic into your daily life. It is a contented happiness, possibly on a regular basis. It is focusing on what you love, and not spending energy on things that drain you or make you feel miserable. It is feeling deep within your bones your purpose, or a solid foundation of working toward finding what helps you feel content with your days as you fall asleep at night. It is feeling at your very core, a strong flicker of positivity that continues, despite being battered by life's challenges.

What does it feel like, on any given day? It is having a morning cup of coffee or tea, hands wrapped about your mug, feeling centered and content. It is performing rituals and taking magical action to bring what you desire into your life. It is reaching out to your community, volunteering in a cause you feel passionate about, and feeling the love and care of your "vibe tribe." It is gardening, cooking, and protecting your home and hearth. It is a reciprocal relationship with your deities in which they help guide you as you step forward in life. It is knowing that your foundation of Paganism is the bonding you feel with nature, daily actions, and community. It is feeling love and loving yourself, no matter your relationship status.

How to begin? As with any foundation, there are a few fundamental building blocks of being a Positive Pagan:

- Making a Choice

- Meditation

- Hydration

- Grounding and Shielding

- Gratitude

- Thinking of Others

I call these building blocks my Positive Pagan tool kit. What follows are a few ideas or rituals to incorporate these foundations (or "tools") into your daily life. If you already do any or all of these practices, wonderful! Perhaps you can incorporate my suggestions, or it can inspire you to revisit these practices if they have lapsed from your day-to-day activities.

The word ritual can sometimes seem daunting. You may think it has to involve lots of different and special items, or you worry that you may say the words wrong, or you don't know the proper order of how to do one. Yes, there are some rituals like that, and we honor them for their complexity and beauty. I consider what I have included as Positive Pagan rituals as generally simple and accessible, so they are easily added to your routine with room for your personal touches.

MAKING A CHOICE

The first fundamental tenet of being a Positive Pagan is simply this: making a choice. Yes, making a choice to be a Positive Pagan is something to do every day. There will be days you forget, and days you are feeling anything but positive and that is perfectly okay. We all have those kinds of days. Don't be hard on yourself if the last thing you want to do upon waking up is be positive. Take the day off. It's perfectly fine.

Think of making a choice as taking back the power and control in your own life. If you use the analogy of swimming in the sea, you can be treading water, and the waves can buffet. But consider this: say you wake up, feeling cranky and out of sorts. You wish you could hide your head under the covers and make the next several hours disappear. As all your internal cylinders start firing, and before you go through the motions of your daily routine, I suggest you stop for a few seconds. Pause. Make time for the Positive Choice Ritual.

Positive Choice Ritual

Items Needed:

Yourself, at the start of your day

A few moments of your time

Upon waking up, take a few moments to do a self-scan. How are you feeling? How is your body feeling? Are you not feeling great? Is yesterday weighing on you, or the week ahead seems daunting? Are your personal interactions weighing heavily upon you?

If yes, then start searching for the glimmer of something positive somewhere deep within you. Maybe your favorite Sabbat on the Wheel of the Year is coming up, or it looks to be a sunny or rainy day (whichever makes you happy), or your best friend is supposed to give you a call later. Those positive glimmers may seem a bit wispy, but I urge you to grab on to them and create a visual bouquet out of them.

Next, I want you to make a choice firmly and clearly to be positive. Say the words to yourself and set the intention. *Example: I choose to be positive today. I choose to see the light during this day. I choose to do what's for the highest good for me and all those I encounter on this day.* It doesn't matter if you feel a bit weird saying it to yourself or out loud. Now smile. The act of smiling relaxes the muscles and releases some tension in your body. Feel that? Now take three deep breaths.

If the entire day seems too daunting, start small. Aim for being positive just during the morning. Grab your morning beverage, or your toothbrush if you brush

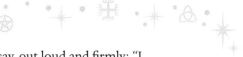

your teeth first thing, and say, out loud and firmly: "I am making a choice to be positive today!"

You may think you sound ridiculous, or you'd prefer to say it internally, so do either. Then pause. Take notice of your body at that moment. Are you clenched up and tense? Take a deep breath, unclench your shoulders, and then check again. Are you frowning? Loosen up that jaw and attempt a tiny smile. Even laugh at yourself for saying those words if you'd like. It may seem a bit ridiculous to be talking to yourself, and that's okay. Check again. Is your body feeling less tense? Take a deep breath. And another. Now, feel the difference from a few moments ago. That is your resistance melting away. That feeling of release is letting go, no matter how briefly you experience it. This may sound like it takes a long time, but it takes a few minutes out of your day at most as you practice these steps.

Now, if you are not used to releasing like this, you may immediately tense up again. What you are feeling might be your need for control, so take a deep breath and try again to loosen up your body. It may take a bit of practice, so don't worry if you don't feel that release on your first try. You may have been experiencing the control pattern for a very long time, so don't expect immediate changes if that is the case. But if you are open to this exercise, it may feel a bit like relief, that pause of release. When you are in that "less tense" moment, try saying the statement about your making a choice to be positive again. Does it resonate with you differently now? If it does, it is time to move onward with your day.

MEDITATION

Do you meditate? Is that a groan I hear? I have suffered from an active, busy mind most of my life. My thoughts darted everywhere, and were rarely reined in, so meditation often ended up being a frustrating experience, so I gave up pretty quickly. I tried desperately to go to my happy place (which changed constantly, of course) and I would be there for a bit, but then ran off again with lists of things I had to do. Or conduct conversations in my head of things I wish I had said. Or think about plans for the next six months of my life. I would do anything to avoid sitting still. Sound familiar?

The first step in any meditation is to be aware of your breathing. That's it. It's amazing how little we notice our breathing, unless someone else points it out. Do you ever get enthused when talking, then shallow breathing kicks in, and before you know it, you feel like you have run a marathon? Deep, satisfying breathing can be achieved by being still, and slowly counting to four every time you inhale and exhale, with a pause in between. In through your nose, and out through your mouth. Not a fast one-two-three-four, but a measured one … two … three … four, with "one Mississippi" length between each number. Stop what you're doing right now. Unclench your shoulders and take some really deep four-part breaths.

How does that feel? Sometimes it helps to set timers on your phone during the day to remind you to breathe. See if that helps. Or try to remember to stop and breathe at the top of every hour.

Once you get comfortable with remembering to breathe deeply for a few days, give meditation another try.

Start off simply at first, for only a few minutes. If thoughts pop up, don't strain against wanting them to go away. Just let them come and go. Don't attach to any of them and try not to let the thoughts spiral into stressful paths. Just mentally sit back and observe the thoughts. Imagine each thought as a bubble, and as it bubbles up, it floats up and pops. It may take you a while to feel detached from those thoughts because we've heard for so long that we need to keep our mind blank during meditation. I have found that removing that idea really helps me relax when thoughts bubble up. We are human, and some days it's hard to turn off that mental switch. Give yourself a mental hug, and let your thoughts float by.

Next, focus on a word, a mantra you've used in the past, a visual point, or a mental view of your favorite place. You can call that place "home" and use that word. Most people are familiar with "om," so you can try that or an intention that you want to set, such as "Peace" or "Love." Just focus on the sound of the word you have chosen, and feel the breath move through your body. Extend your time as you get used to this routine and try it a bit longer each day for at least a week. Then take notice and note the differences. Life might feel calmer, events don't seem as stressful, and the edges of life don't feel quite so jangly.

If meditation doesn't come easily, or you struggle with it, then find teachers or a group of fellow meditators. Many communities offer classes and there are online options, phone apps (I highly recommend Insight Timer), and YouTube videos. Some may prefer meditative music or guided meditation, so explore all available options to see what suits you and your life.

If you still don't think you can squeeze meditation in because life is too busy, then consider waking up earlier. Can you spare twenty minutes before you check your phone, make your morning beverage, or switch on the television? Find parts of your day that you can add this time, as it's only a fraction of the day, and the benefits are wonderful. In a 24-hour day, there are 1,440 minutes. If you meditate 20 minutes twice daily, that still leaves 1,400 minutes in which to live your life. Consider it a gift to yourself that you receive twice a day.

Start out with smaller increments of time if mediation seems too daunting. Aim for five minutes at first. Make it something enjoyable so it's not an activity you dread. Sit in a cozy spot, surrounded by items you love. Play some soothing music if you feel that would help. Designate a shawl, sweater, or cozy shirt to wear during meditation so you feel comfortable and relaxed. Perhaps there is a beaded necklace or bracelet you can hold while you meditate that feels comforting. Ask a friend to meditate with you, locally or long distance, and try to meditate daily for at least a week.

Meditation is one of the most used tools in the Positive Pagan tool kit. If you are really struggling with meditation, then try waking up early for just one day and focus only on spending time in the quiet. Watch the sun rise, and enjoy a soothing, warm beverage. Put off thinking about what is on your to-do list, and just be quiet and still in the moment.

How did that feel? Was it soothing and cozy? If yes, then that is what meditation can feel like. If you enjoyed the quiet comfort of the morning, then continue doing it as a gateway to the meditation practices I previously outlined.

If none of these suggestions work for you, put it to one side and give it a try at another time. Sometimes circumstances in your life shift to allow other things into being, and the same holds true for meditation.

HYDRATION

Hydration is essential for positive feelings. Our bodies are made of 60 percent water, so it makes sense that water itself helps keep us in a positive state. That positive flow you can feel is enhanced by drinking water. There have been studies that have shown water crystals are negatively affected by screaming or yelling, whereas beautiful water crystals were formed from positive language and uplifting music. Makes sense, doesn't it?

Some find drinking water boring or challenging because it is so tasteless.

A few suggestions:

- Use a glass or steel water bottle, not plastic. Having your hydration in a natural container helps the environment. If you find yourself using a plastic bottle, be sure to recycle.

- Say some positive words over your water as you fill your reusable water bottle.

- Place some uplifting or protective stickers on your water bottle.

- Every time you fill your water bottle, place your hand over it, sending it energy with thoughts and words of gratitude.

- Add natural flavor enhancers to your water such as cucumber, mint leaves, lemon, or ginger.

GROUNDING AND SHIELDING

Grounding and shielding are two very important components of the Positive Pagan tool kit. To ground and shield yourself is as simple as the words imply: you ground yourself to the earth to help be present in the moment and not float away into your thoughts or elsewhere. Shielding can feel as if you are holding up an invisible shield to protect you from other people's energy. I strongly recommend grounding and shielding daily before you face the world. Yes, sometimes you will forget, but a regular rotation of both practices will enable you to ground quickly and get shields into place.

If you are not familiar with grounding, there are a few simple techniques that are quick and effective. One method is to sit still, close your eyes with your feet flat on the floor, and imagine roots growing out of the bottoms of your feet and deep into the ground. Go beyond the floor, the basement, and the foundation of where you are, and deep into the earth below. Once you feel connected to the earth, let all the sludge in your body (emotional, mental, residual) flow down, past the floor, down as deep as you can imagine. Consider it spiritual compost, sending it down to the deepest part of the earth. Once you feel this action is complete, take a deep breath and open your eyes.

Grounding feels as if you have solid, comfortable, heavyweight shoes so you feel more attached to the earth itself, instead of a mental floating sensation. You know that feeling when you're distracted and your mind is elsewhere, or in a hundred different places? Grounding is the opposite.

If you need a quick, effective method, do the following: walk barefoot on a patch of grass outside. If you are unable to go outside, no problem! Run your fingers through the dirt of a potted plant. It's always helpful to have at least a plant or two in your home for this purpose.

Another quick technique is to wear a hematite ring. Hematite has very strong grounding energy and protective qualities, so wearing it in jewelry ensures you are covered in both these areas, especially if you find yourself around a lot of people during the course of your day. If you don't like wearing jewelry, then carry a hematite stone in your pocket. I recommend keeping the stone (or stones) in a small cotton or mesh bag so it's more prominent, and then you will remember to take it out of your pocket before washing your clothes.

Black tourmaline is also a good stone to keep on hand, as it is also known for its grounding and protection properties. I find it useful to keep a stone or two at my desk, or when I work in a public setting, to keep the energy clear around me. It's a stone that feels good to touch as well, as stroking its ridges can be soothing if done repetitively.

While crystals and stones are known to have specific purposes, I recommend you go with what feels the most grounding to you. If you have a go-to crystal, keep it handy. Finding what grounds you can change as you go through life, and finding what it is can be a trial-and-error process. It could be a different personal object or an item found in nature. When hiking or walking outdoors, gather a few nuts, stones, and twigs from the ground as a quick grounding method. Hold them in your hand, take a few deep breaths, and focus on the energy you feel within these items.

Other ways of grounding include hugging a tree. If you've not done this before, fully embrace a tree. If you are very still, notice the tree's energy. Each tree has a different vitality, and it is a wonderful way to feel connected when in nature.

Shielding can take on many forms, whether you visualize yourself surrounded by mirrors, opaque walls, or vibrant gemstone barriers. The walls can be reflective or visualize something akin to the tinted windows in a car. I don't recommend boxing yourself off with a roof or ceiling, as the purpose of shielding is exactly that: to keep unwanted energy away from you, not to keep you completely contained. Sometimes people forget this detail, and it can result in your energy feeling trapped and stagnant.

You can also shield yourself with white light or envision your ancestors' love surrounding you. I have also visualized holding up a shield (similar to a medieval shield) to reflect negative energy. Another option is to pull down positive energy from your deities, have it flow through you, and then flow outward (similar to how a light projector works) to keep unwanted negative energy at bay.

If you prefer a physical object to help you feel shielded, then I recommend a spell bag filled with your protective crystals and some nettle, as this is the combination I've found useful as a protective energy as I go about my day. A spell bag is a simple cotton bag, or you can use a small cloth handkerchief. Place it in a pocket or somewhere in your clothing where it won't be dislodged.

Practice shielding as often as you can, ideally daily, until it becomes as easy as snapping your fingers to visualize the shielding barriers going up around. Daily or regular practice will help this become part of your day, but please be patient with yourself if you don't feel you've mastered it immediately.

How does shielding feel? How will you know if you are doing it correctly? It may feel like an invisible barrier protecting against incoming negative or frenetic energy. If you find yourself around persistent toxic or negative energy, shielding can sometimes feel difficult to maintain on a consistent basis. When that happens, it is a clear signal to step away physically if you can, regroup, do some deep breathing, and replenish those shields. If this happens in a work situation, and it continues, consider it a sign to start looking for another job if you can. If you immediately say, "That's impossible!" note the word possible within that phrase. Being a Positive Pagan means embracing the idea that many things are possible.

With a regular practice of grounding and shielding, it should happen so automatically that you don't even think about it. But if you are going about your day and notice that you forgot, just stop and take the time to ground and shield immediately. Consider it as important as brushing your teeth and putting on your seatbelt!

GRATITUDE

This part of your Positive Pagan tool kit is very simple: Be grateful.

"Grateful" is a word that gets thrown around a lot and can lose its meaning if you don't pause and really consider what the word conveys. Being grateful by itself is not enough, just as one brick isn't enough to build a foundation. Gratitude is one of many bricks, but it's a mighty one.

Start with the basics. You can wake up, and instead of reaching for your phone, spend a few minutes mentally checking your body. As you inwardly scan yourself, be grateful for your senses, for breathing, for your body, and for your abilities.

Are there more things you are grateful for? Write them down or mentally list them. If it helps, keep a gratitude notebook or notepad by your bed if this is a practice you'd like to start or end your day with. Start with one to three gratitude items a day and increase as necessary. It's a wonderful exercise to start your day in a positive mind frame. It's also okay to repeat items on your gratitude list. List whatever makes your heart sing or has you feeling quietly content. And if there are days where you struggle to find one thing to be grateful for, then take a break for a few days, and return to the practice later.

There are other ways to incorporate gratitude throughout your day, from simple rituals to more involved ones.

Quick Gratitude Ritual

Items Needed:
Yourself and your choice of item to stir
A few moments of your time

A simple and effective method of expressing gratitude is the act of stirring. You can do this ritual with your morning coffee/tea, when you cook or bake, or when you mix anything into a beverage. Stir in multiples of three (three, six, nine, etc.) and offer a silent gratitude for the day. Three is considered a magical number for many reasons, including Maiden, Mother, Crone; the symbol of the triskele; and the grouping of past, present, and future. You can always choose to stir however many times you like, but adding a little dose of the magical number three can set the intention for your day while adding a bit of magic to this seemingly mundane action.

Gratitude Altar

Items Needed:

Small table or shelf
Items you're grateful for

A Gratitude Altar doesn't need to take up much space. You can use a small table, a shelf in a bookcase, the top of a bookcase, a mantelpiece, a kitchen windowsill, or a basket. The most important feature is that it should be easily accessible, and in a space where you see it daily.

On or in it, place items that you're grateful for, either the actual items, or a representation of them. For example, if you are grateful for the abundance in your life, place a few coins or paper play money as a representation. Place items of nature on your Gratitude Altar, photographs, mementos, and more. This is a fun altar to maintain because it is an instant visual boost of what you are grateful for in your life.

Rituals also help deepen the practice of gratitude, so here is a ritual I like to perform at least quarterly. This is also a good ritual to use around Thanksgiving, or any of the harvest celebrations (Lammas/Lughnasadh, Mabon/Autumn Equinox, and Samhain).

Positive Pagan Gratitude Ritual

Items Needed:

Small table, shelf, or box
Scarf or vibrantly colored cloth (optional)
Your Gratitude Journal (This can be a plain note-
*   book, a stack of sticky notes, or a very decorative*
*   journal in which you record what you're grateful*
*   for on a regular basis)*
Glass of water
Flower(s) in a vase (dried flowers also work well)

Small piece of your favorite art or poetry
Piece of rose quartz
Items from nature (bark, leaves, sea shells, rocks, etc.)

To perform this ritual, pick your favorite part of the day to perform this ritual, whether it's early morning, midday, or evening. On a dedicated table, shelf, or box, place all items from the list.

Ground and center yourself. Deeply breathe in through your nose and out through your mouth six to nine times, hold the piece of rose quartz, and imagine walking barefoot through grass or picture yourself in a canoe in the middle of a calm lake. Breathe in these peaceful moments and take note of what you see around you.

Spend five to ten minutes in this space each day, writing down a list of the things, people, places, and items you are grateful for. They can include food, beverages, moments, presents, mail you received, or people who brightened your day. Don't limit yourself, nor pressure yourself into thinking anything listed must be spectacular. There is quiet joy in the little things in life.

> Now, take a moment to view all the items on your altar, noting each one, and what it means to you.
> Drink the water, and say your affirmation three times:
>
> *My thanks for what is now, what will be, and has been. I will look with fresh eyes for more today to be grateful for tomorrow.*
>
> Take a deep breath, place your hand on your heart, and feel your gratitude.
>
> When you feel complete, move onward with your day.

Gratitude Memory Jar

Items Needed:

Small jar

Pen and pieces of paper

During the course of your days, if you feel grateful about an event, happening, or person, write down the memory on a piece of paper and add it to your Gratitude Jar. You can open the jar monthly, quarterly, or at the end of the year. It's a useful tool to look back on things you may have overlooked and is especially helpful if you feel like you haven't accomplished or experienced anything at all, or if you don't keep a diary or journal. You accomplish and experience more than you think you do! Get creative with your jar and make it something that you will enjoy contributing to during the course of time you decide upon: monthly, quarterly, on Samhain, or New Year's Eve.

Gratitude Wall

Items Needed:

Dry erase board or wall covered in chalk paint,
  along with the coordinating writing tool

Sticky notes, pins, and a bulletin board

If you want your gratitude in a place where you can see it, then consider painting one wall with chalk paint, and write on it when you feel moved by gratitude. Think about it: a whole wall filled with your words of gratitude. What a visual feast!

Dry erase boards are also useful, and you can even cover the wall with self-adhesive whiteboard wall material. You can also pin sticky notes to a bulletin board or cover a wall with sticky notes. Try index cards in a recipe box or get some flat stones to write on and place them in a clear vase. Get creative and see where in your home you would like to express your daily gratitude. Be sure to place your creation where you can see it every day. Consider leaving it unfinished so you can add to it as the year winds onward.

THINKING OF OTHERS

You may feel you already think of others in the course of your day, especially if you have close friends or family. This part of being a Positive Pagan takes a bit of self-reflection. In the course of any given day, do you regularly think of others? Or do you feel as if you are caught up in your own life, and that you will get to thinking of others at a later time, a time that never seems convenient? If your life is harried and hectic, and you have no room for others in your life, I ask that you pause for a few moments.

Is there a way you can include thinking of others in your daily activities? It can be as simple as sending a text to a friend to check on them. Reaching out to someone you haven't heard from in a while to see how they are doing. Perhaps your community participates in regular volunteer work that you participate in, or you volunteer at your child's school or a cause that is dear to your heart. This foundation of being a Positive Pagan shouldn't feel like a burden. It's a physical and mental act of reaching outward in your world, with the goal of helping others and your community. Positive Paganism includes looking outside of ourselves on a regular basis to ask "How can I help?" and finding ways to do so.

If this thought process seems unfamiliar to you, start slowly to see how it feels. Start by bringing your co-worker a treat or look into volunteering for a cause that means a lot to you. Not sure of what causes you feel drawn to? Sit down with some paper and list some areas that are important to you: animals, the environment, education, politics, etc. There may not be a whole lot of free time in your schedule, so donating items from your home, making online donations, or finding online volunteering options could be helpful options.

Why think of others? How is this a foundation of being a Positive Pagan? Well, we don't live in a bubble, so our actions can affect the world around us. What you put out will come back to you, so reaching out to others not only has the effect of making you feel good, but it will also reflect back to you in other ways. The person you help may introduce you to a future best friend or lead to a new job or career. The positive energy you put into volunteering will not only help with your action, but it may also inspire others to volunteer as well. Many hands helping involves action, and action invariably helps us feel better mentally. If we are feeling better mentally, that leads to an ease in being a Positive Pagan. There is truly nothing negative about thinking of others, unless you feel it is a huge burden and unmanageable to you. If that happens, then stop and try again later. A different frame of mind might lead to an easier transition to this foundation.

POSITIVE PAGAN JOURNAL

Now that you have established a foundation and the basics of the Positive Pagan tool kit, it is time to add a journal to your activities. Throughout this book, I will ask a few questions to reflect upon as you travel on this journey of being a Positive Pagan.

The journal can be as fancy or as simple as you would like. It can be a notebook from your local drugstore or a leather-bound journal and quill pens. Find something that really pleases you to use, as its purpose is to be a companion to this book.

Remember old-fashioned maps? This journal will be a written record of your journey as a Positive Pagan. Parts of the road may seem familiar, or it may be all-new territory. As you go on your journey as a Positive Pagan, add notes, lists, creative musings, venting sessions, mementos, photographs, collages, quotes, and more. Other options include writing notes into your phone, discussing them with a close friend or confidant, or adding your answers to an online journal.

You may want to read this book from cover to cover, and then go back to answer the questions. Or you may like to pause when you get to a journal prompt. Whichever way you choose, the journal is meant to be a positive addition to reading and using this book.

Positive Pagan Book and Journal Ritual

Here is a ritual to consecrate both this book and your journal.

Items Needed:

Your journal

This book, Positive Pagan

A candle and matches

Your favorite incense

A bell

Your favorite crystal

Begin this ritual in your favorite place at home. It can be your bedroom, in the kitchen, or by your favorite chair.

Place all the items for the ritual in a circle around the book.

Place the journal underneath the book.

Light the candle and the incense.

Close your eyes.

Breathe deeply three times.

Open your eyes and ring the bell nine times to move any residual energy away from the book and journal.

Place one hand on the books and one hand on your heart.

Say some words about the journey you are going to undertake. It can be something as simple as *I begin this journey into Positive Paganism with clear intent, and a willing heart. So mote it be.* Some people prefer if their words rhyme, so you can use, *Positive Pagan, a journey to start, may this book become, in the days ahead, my own hearth and heart.* Both are examples, but if you are so moved, please use your own language and words to personalize this ritual.

Next, place your favorite crystal upon the books.

Rub your hands together to create some energy and hold them over the crystal and books.

Send energy downward to the crystal and books.

Close your eyes, envisioning using the books to enhance your life.

Place one hand over your heart, taking three deep breaths.

This is a gift you give yourself.

Follow this ritual with a favorite beverage and snack. There! Now your book and journal are consecrated and ready to use.

There are a few uses for an herb bundle in consecrating items and clearing energy in this book. If you don't have one readily available, here is an option you can utilize when needed!

Positive Pagan Herb Bundle

Items Needed:
Herbs (thyme, lavender, and rosemary)
Embroidery thread
Lighter

Ceramic bowl or abalone/any large shell
Feather

Harvest or purchase the herbs, and then proceed with drying them. Let them wilt somewhere dry for at least twenty-four hours, preferably longer.

Bunch them tightly into a bundle and tie the ends with embroidery threads using a tight knot. Continue wrapping the thread around the herbs a few more times and finish with a second knot. Start at the other end, if needed, and repeat the process.

Once you have a satisfactory bundle, place your right hand on the herbs, sending positive energy into them, saying the words of the intent you wish to set for your herb bundle. For example, *May this bundle of herbs send positive and loving energy throughout my home, with protection for those who pass through its doorways.* Hang the bundle in a sunny window or dry place for a few more weeks until dry.

When you are ready to use the bundle, hold it close to your heart again, sending the intent of positivity and protection into it (consider it a top-off of magical energy). Carefully light one end, and as it catches on fire, blow out the flame. There should be glowing embers, but if not, try lighting it again. Hold the bowl or shell beneath the herb bundle to catch any falling embers. If the embers seem like they are burning out, blow upon it to coax it back to life. Use the feather to waft the smoke around as you move around. If a feather is not available, you can use your hand.

Begin to waft the smoke around your space, offering thanks to the plants for offering their own particular magic.

Positive Pagan Journey Ritual

As you can tell, I liken the path to Positive Paganism to a journey. Here is a ritual you can do by yourself as a solitary practitioner, or you can experience this with a group of friends if this is a journey you'd like to undertake together.

Items Needed:

Two candles (tealights or chime candles are great, but use what you have)

Lavender, bay leaf, and sage (approximately a teaspoon of each)

Small bowl

Music that inspires you

8.5 inch x 11 inch piece of paper, unlined

Markers, crayons, or pens

A bell

If possible, perform this ritual on a New Moon. Place the objects in your sacred space, cast your circle, calling in all those who guide you in this life to join you as you begin this journey.

Light your candles.

Mix the herbs in your bowl, running your fingers through the herbs to release their fragrance.

Take a few deep breaths to center and ground yourself.

Play some music that inspires you.

Eyes closed, begin to see yourself how YOU want to be as a Positive Pagan.

Notice every detail, from what you're wear to your surroundings.

Notice your senses in that moment. What are you seeing, feeling, tasting, touching, and hearing?

Once you feel content with that image, open your eyes.

Take your paper and art supplies and draw a map of that image. Start north with the top of your head, and move your way downward to the south, filling in east and west. It can be a drawing of yourself, or representations of what you will do to arrive at that image (clothes, ritual items, herbs, actions, etc.). Be as creative as you'd like!

This does not need to be a finished product; you can update it as you move through the exercises in this book.

When done, ring the bell over it in all four directions.

Open your circle and follow with a nourishing snack and favorite beverage.

You can leave the herbs on your altar as an offering or place a bit of them in a small cotton bag to carry with you in your bag/purse/briefcase or in your car as a reminder of your journey.

Journal Prompt

So, now it's time for your first journal entry! Get out your Positive Pagan journal and ponder the following:

List ten things you can do to add positivity to your life. They can be small changes to your routine or ways of being that you would like to add to your life.

Additional Thoughts

Are any of these difficult or challenging? Which ones are you looking forward to? Include any thoughts or ruminations you had while reading this first chapter. Did you get inspired to look into volunteer work?

2

Tools and Supplies

As a Positive Pagan, you won't require a shopping list of new items, because you may already use several tools in the following list in your own spiritual practice. Many items may seem familiar to you, or you may add some items to your next shopping adventure to a metaphysical store or online shop. I will list many of the items I have found useful in my journey of being a Positive Pagan. I have used all of them and find them a necessary part of my personal tool kit. They are in alphabetical order for easy reference. As with other aspects of this book, give things a try if they resonate with you, or bookmark them for later use.

ALTAR

An altar can be something as simple as a bookshelf or small table; any flat surface will do. If you don't have any space you can give up, consider a solid wooden shoe rack, as it sits low to the ground, usually has one shelf for storage, and is unobtrusive and sturdy. I have used the top of a desk, a shelf in a bookcase, and kept items in a wooden box to use while traveling. Windowsills are good in a pinch, and a wooden tray is also useful because you can move it around as needed. What's most important in altars is that they reflect YOU and what you like best. I use the term "resonate" quite a bit in this book because it is important to really go with your intuition or gut feeling as to what you want to place on your altar. Otherwise it ends up becoming a collection of items that gather dust. Your altar can be focused on your deity or deities, change with the seasons, or get updated for every celebration on the Wheel of the Year. An altar is a focal point, a place to spend time with your deity/ deities, and it should be a calm oasis if your life is feeling chaotic.

If you already have an altar, use this entry as a reminder to dust it off, clean off your objects, and change up the energy by creating a fresh, new vista. It is important to keep the energy clear around an altar, as it can become stagnant and impersonal.

There are many "Altar Building 101" classes online and in-person, so take some time to seek your inspiration. If you are not sure where you'd like to begin, a starting point is to represent all the elements with an object on your altar. Here are a few examples:

North/Earth A small bowl of local dirt, or sand, gravel, or dirt from a place special to you is a wonderful addition. Or add a favorite stone or crystal, items from nature you pick up during a walk, a seashell from the beach, or an item from your previous home that feels centering and grounding.

East/Air All aspects of air, from feathers, bells, small musical instruments, incense, wind chimes, streamers, to pictures of birds and toy airplanes can be used. Bubbles are a whimsical addition as well. What represents air to you? Perhaps a photo of clouds or a fallen leaf during autumn?

South/Fire The element of fire, such as matches, lighters, candles, lamps, or dragons, as well as cacti and crushed red pepper flakes are all good representations of the element of fire.

West/Water Water can be represented by any liquid in a cup, whether it be water itself, wine, or a different preferred alcohol. Rainwater, holy water, or water from a lake, beach, or ocean would also be lovely additions. Seashells, driftwood, or a favorite photo of the ocean could be good representations as well.

There is no wrong way to set up your altar, so begin with the elements or something simple like a candle or a rock you found outside and take it from there. What matters is the intention with which you set up your altar. Keep that in mind and see what you create!

ALTAR CLOTHS

You don't have to get a fancy, specific altar cloth for your altar, unless it is really important to you to have a certain style. Inexpensive substitutes include bandanas or fabric remnants, which are usually found in craft or dollar stores. It's nice to have a covering for the surface so there won't be scratches from items placed on the altar, but you can also remedy that by using small plates or leaves underneath. You can also create an altar cloth with a solid-colored piece of material and draw symbols and/or words that are meaningful for you.

BELLS

Bells are great as a quick method of moving energy when you don't have much time or focus to do so otherwise. Ring a bell to dispel negative energy, freshen up the energy around your altar, or to have a quick refresh when you need it. You can have a handbell on your altar or a string of bells on your door handle or window, all useful to change the energy as well. Wear bells on an ankle bracelet and keep one available in your car for clearing energy when needed.

BLACK SALT

Black salt is an important and basic component for use in protection spells and banework, so I recommend always keeping some on hand. It is fairly common to find this item in metaphysical shops or online, but if you'd like to make your own, here is a simple recipe I have used in between my own supply runs:

Black Salt Recipe
Items Needed:
Coarse, natural salt (kosher or sea salt is fine)
Any of the following:
Fire pit ash, black pepper, incense ash, natural
black food coloring

Combine the items above until it is the color you like and store in an airtight container.

Consider using the energy of the Dark Moon to make your own black salt, as it will help with its magical properties. For easy reference, the Dark Moon is the evening before a New Moon. (If you aren't sure of when the New Moon will be, Google "next new moon," download a moon app, or look at a *Farmers' Almanac* or a calendar.)

BOOKS

Part of being a Positive Pagan is expanding our knowledge base and being curious about the world around us. No matter what your practice, there is always more to learn. People have different perspectives, practices, and knowledge that they share, and it can be useful as inspiration for your own practice. If you are interested in certain spiritual pathways, want to know more about your deity / deities, or learn different forms of divination, increase your library. Books are just one of many ways to gain knowledge, so other ways of gathering information are included in this category, including magazines, research/finding information online, and audiobooks.

Books, especially nonfiction, are also good for perspective, because you learn about other people's way of life and practices. If you keep an open mind and heart while reading about others' struggles and lessons, you can find some nugget in there to inspire or help if you find yourself in similar situations. Be inspired by those who have gone before and share their wisdom; it can light your pathway when you least expect it.

CANDLES

Candles are so useful and frankly necessary for a Positive Pagan. Not only do they provide a soothing light, they also are beneficial for spellwork and meditation. Chime candles and seven-day candles are useful to have on hand, and colors correspond with magical intentions. A quick checklist of colors and their magical focus includes:

White Great for clearing old energies, promoting serenity and peace, and is useful for personal insight. It can also be used in place of the other colors for magical intent if you don't have that color available.

Black Useful for protection and warding off negative energies.

Yellow Associated with abundance and joy, and is also useful for new social and job networking opportunities. Keep a yellow candle in your desk or work area for a work boost.

Orange Not just for Halloween! Use this color for creative boosts when you're feeling stuck and uninspired.

Green Helps amplify abundance and growth.

Blue Connects with peace and protection. It's also useful for communication spells and dealing with emotional wounds.

Red For love, passion, and the color of action and energy.

Chime candles are small, so they're very useful if you want to do quick spellwork. Blowing out a candle ends the "work" of the candle's focus, so be sure to have a snuffer on hand, if possible. Snuffing out a candle allows you to use the candle for continued work on a spell. Seven-day candles are best used for long-term spell workings, and while their name implies you can burn it continuously for seven days, you should place the candle in a safe spot such as sink or bathtub. If you are not comfortable with a continuously burning candle, I recommend lighting the candle at the same time each day, for the same amount of time, for a predetermined number of days. For example, if you want to work on a spell for seven days, then you would light the candle for an hour each evening for seven days. Again, the focus is on the intention, so whether or not you keep the candle lit for seven days continuously or an hour for seven days is less important than the intent behind it.

Birthday candles are also good to have on hand for when time is limited and it's necessary to have the candle burn out completely. Due to their small size, you can accomplish this without too much fuss.

The Shabbat candles found in the kosher or Jewish food section of your grocery store are also useful, as they are white and therefore convenient for all kinds of workings. They also burn cleanly and relatively quickly, within a few hours, and are very sturdy.

CAULDRON

Cauldrons are useful for spellwork, as they are a safe container for burning herbs, small papers, and loose incense. Small ones are usually affordable, and those with a lid are especially useful for extinguishing flames when they get a bit too robust. Also take a look at antique shops or estate sales, as some have cauldrons as family heirlooms, even if they were previously used for other purposes. Cauldrons are a wonderful addition for setting sacred space, clearing energy, and processing endings. As with other items, take some time searching for your cauldron. Touch it with your hands, feel its energy, and wait to envision it in your life. Be sure to cleanse the previous owner's energy of your cauldron (even if purchased brand new in a shop) with smoke or salt.

CRYSTALS

There are a few crystals I keep in rotation as part of my Positive Pagan tool kit. Those listed here are just a few of the amazing crystals out there, and I encourage you to learn more and visit crystal shops to see what calls to you. I have often found when a crystal catches my eye, it ends up being because I needed it for a particular use. Look up metaphysical properties of any crystal you buy and see if that happens to you! Many shops provide information with any crystal you purchase, and while buying online is an option, it is a wonderful sensory experience to choose the stones yourself.

Citrine A great stone for motivation, creative endeavors, and releasing negativity. A positive, sunny looking stone, it is a quick mood boost when you need it.

Clear Quartz Used for harmony, clarity, and calmness. A clear quartz feels good when you hold it and is known as a healing stone.

Dumortierite Known for helping to increase patience and stimulate intellectual abilities. I keep this one handy for mental clarity and when I hit a mental wall. It also helps amplify your intuitive gifts, so if you are feeling a bit stagnant in that area, find this stone. It is very useful for those days when you feel less than confident in thoughts and actions.

Garnet This stone is known for revitalizing, balancing, and energizing. Its reddish color is warm and comforting and is also good for alleviating emotional discomfort.

Hematite I am never without my hematite because it has a strong grounding energy. It is also known to help with concentration and focus.

Lapis Lazuli This stone is great for revealing one's inner truths, and also helps stimulate clarity. A great stone to hold when you are feeling the effects of brain fog or want a quick boost to get back to your centered self. I like to use this stone while meditating.

Lepidolite I find this stone the most useful for when I feel scattered and frazzled. It is a very soothing stone, and one I turn to during chaotic times in my life.

Ocean Jasper This is a stone I use most when I feel under the weather or sad. This stone helps relieve stress and inspires happiness, along with feelings of protection. I like to use this stone for releasing negative emotions and thought patterns.

Rose Quartz I call this my Love Crystal. It's useful when there is strife in friendships, or when your self-esteem takes a hit. It inspires feelings of peace and harmony. I like to use this stone when I'm in a stressful environment, so I always keep it nearby.

Selenite Selenite is great to quickly clear the energy from any of my crystals. I also like to use it for meditation, as it inspires clarity.

Tourmaline Tourmaline is known for its protective energy, and for repelling negativity. I find it to be a very calming stone and useful for releasing tension. If I've had a stressful day, I like to hold this stone in my hand while meditating.

As with all stones and crystals, be sure to cleanse them before use, either with sunlight, incense, or wildcrafted herbal smoke. Remember to charge them under the Full Moon when you can and take some time to really feel the energy of the stones.

Many times we purchase crystals because they are beautiful, and that is perfectly fine! You may not be drawn to crystals or stones for their metaphysical use, but do have a cursory knowledge of their properties. If you use them later for spellwork or for a specific intention, be sure you cleanse and charge them. Also, be aware that having a large pile of stones and crystals in your room may emit some chaotic energy. (Imagine different streams of energy emanating from each of them, all at once!) Rotate your display and keep some in storage so they are not all out at the same time.

DIVINATION TOOLS

Do you practice a form of divination? Tarot cards, oracle cards, Lenormand or Kipper cards, pendulums, scrying, or something else? Cloud, fire, or smoke scrying? Divination is a wonderful tool to help with life's vagaries, and another tool that is part of the Positive Pagan tool kit. If you are not familiar with the different forms of divination, then be sure to explore them. Get readings from a variety of divinations, from cards to palm reading, psychic mediums, astrologers, and scryers. Explore it all and see what you like and feel comfortable with to experience and practice.

FLORIDA WATER

I am a huge fan of Florida Water! If you are not familiar with this item, it is an American version of eau de cologne, otherwise known as Cologne Water. The name itself refers to the Fountain of Youth.

As with everything I list in this book, it's important that you feel comfortable with its usage. If you are not, then no need to add it to your tools and supplies.

The Fountain of Youth, which was thought to be located in Florida, is often used by southern practitioners of hoodoo and voodoo. It can usually be found at your local metaphysical shop or online. It has a light, pleasant smell, and is useful in cleansing your personal space.

Florida Water Cleansing Ritual

Go into each room and sprinkle Florida Water in all four corners, accompanied by the following words:

"Peace and protection, may it be found here!

May all who enter this room feel harmony and contentment."

Use whatever words you feel comfortable using, with a different intention for each room, if you would like to do so. What matters is the intent you have for this cleansing: Is it for protection? Clearing the energy? Bringing in peacefulness? Be clear about your intention before you begin so your working is effective.

You can find recipes for Florida Water online, so if you would prefer to make your own, by all means do so. Using native plants and alcohol will add a personal component, which can be very powerful.

HERBS

As with crystals, there are a few herbs I use as a Positive Pagan. I am by no means an herbalist, but I do enjoy adding to my knowledge about herbs and their uses. Many of the following herbs are probably already found in your kitchen cabinet, so no need for a huge investment. This is not a comprehensive list, but rather a few basics I always have in use with my spellwork and daily life:

Basil I use basil to repel negative energies, for positive financial outcomes, and for prosperity.

Bay Leaves A good herb to use for protection, healing, setting intentions, and purification.

Cinnamon Another great herb for protection. I recommend having both ground and cinnamon sticks in your supplies. A bundle of cinnamon sticks over your door repels negative energy and is also useful for prosperity and abundance workings. The sticks are also useful for charging your divination tools, so throw a stick in your tarot or rune bag and keep a stick near your crystal ball or scrying mirror.

Cloves Cloves are useful for repelling negative energy and for prosperity workings. Also good for bringing in positive spiritual vibrations.

Lavender I call this one my relaxation herb. Useful for fatigue and helps soothe jangled feelings.

Mint Ah, the soothing scent of mint is useful to bring in peacefulness. It is a very healing and calming herb and can also be used to attract prosperity.

Mugwort This herb is useful for lucid dreaming and astral travel. It can also be used for protective energy.

Rosemary I consider this a powerhouse herb because it's useful for so many things. I like to use it when I make cleaning supplies and floor washes. It is also good for purifying and cleansing, and another herb useful for protection. I like to keep it planted around my home space, so keep it in pots, if possible, or at least have one plant in your window.

NATURE SCRYING

In addition to crystal balls and scrying mirrors, you can also scry clouds, fire, or smoke. Cloud scrying is the easiest entry into this form of divination since it's as easy as looking up. Look upward on a cloud-filled day and see what forms or shapes you pick out. Remember doing this as a child? View upward with a sense of wonder and note if the shapes refer to something that's been on your mind. As with any form of divination, it takes interest and practice, so don't get discouraged if you don't see anything right away.

Fire or smoke scrying is also relatively simple and something you can do the next time you enjoy a fire in a firepit or fireplace. Observe the fire and the smoke it makes to ascertain shapes.

If you light incense, observe the smoke as it swirls upward. In addition to helping create a sacred space, the incense smoke might form a silhouette or figure that may resonate with what's in your heart.

If you don't feel called to any form of divination, try to examine why you feel that way. If you feel intimidated, ask a friend to show you how they use divination in their life to see if that helps. No worries if you prefer to not use divination as part of your Positive Pagan tool kit. It's something that can be added later, and there may be a blockage to divination at this point in your life, so revisit when you feel comfortable.

NOTEBOOKS

Notebooks can be a great addition to the Positive Pagan tool kit. They are useful for note-taking during courses and workshops, a place to jot down spellwork ideas, make lists and plans, take quick notations, and even journaling. If you don't have a Book of Shadows, or have no interest in starting one, then use the notebook to keep track of spellwork successes and stalls, shopping lists for tools, and for planning Wheel of the Year celebrations. A Book of Shadows is what some practitioners use to keep track of their rituals and spellwork but is not necessarily used in all traditions. Notebooks are great for working out elements of spellwork or if you want to incorporate different items and you need a comprehensive place to keep all the information together.

You may want to use your notebook to write poetry or prose in honor of your deity / deities, list which offerings you've made so you don't repeat them, or make lists of magical subjects you'd like to learn. The possibilities are endless, and while electronic usage to keep track of ideas is not discouraged, it is a grounding practice to write down thoughts and lists. Start with a small, inexpensive notebook, and keep it nearby. See what you end up using it for and enjoy the process!

PROTECTIVE JEWELRY

The jewelry you wear can be similar to armor if utilized effectively. I find hematite rings to be the easiest way to ward off negative energy, and it also helps with focusing and grounding. Have a favorite pendant? Anoint it with a special oil, either one you make or purchase. The intention can be for protection, grounding, or self-love. Pagans love their jewelry, as it can be their subtle calling card into the world: "Are you one, too?" It's always a nice feeling of community when you are surrounded by others who are on similar paths. The jewelry itself becomes community enhancing. Whether bright and bold or subtle and discreet, your jewelry can be your calling card, your identity, and your protection.

Find a ring that has meaning, possibly engraved with special words that are your mantra. I have a ring with the Sanskrit words for truth, knowledge, and bliss, which I wear as a daily reminder of my goals in life. It is also a memento of an important moment of my spiritual journey, so it has tremendous value to me.

Bracelets can also be used for protection, whether it is made of protective crystals (amber, black tourmaline, rose quartz, amethyst, or malachite are a few that work well), a precious metal or metal mixture that means a great deal to you, or engraved with words that give you strength. Earrings have their own unique protective value, whether singly or in multiples. Ear cuffs shaped like dragons are among my favorite ways to provide subtle protection when I am out and about. Whenever possible, use jewelry made with natural items, and if it has sentimental value, imbuing it with protection oil or energy will work as well.

SOCIAL MEDIA

Social media is a tool? Yes, if you use it wisely. Social media can be a bane and taking breaks from it is highly recommended. Even if you attempt to remove it from all your devices, social media will no doubt creep back into your days. News articles referencing Twitter, or a photo that catches your eye from Instagram, and before you know it, you are back in the thick of it.

Social media is useful as a way to keep in touch if your community and friendships are worldwide. Letter writing or emailing may be preferred, but how easy is it to send a quick message on Facebook? Instagram can be inspiring to see what other people in the world do for their spellwork, altars, and practices. Yet you may start looking at one account, and then another, and before you know it a few hours have disappeared.

If you view social media as a tool, then the power is in your hands, and YOU get to decide the boundaries of usage. Part of the Positive Pagan tool kit is to find ways of energizing yourself, so inspiration can be found on social media, and in turn, energize your practice. Seek your own inspiration in ways that enhance your life. Join Pagan and witchcraft Facebook groups (be sure to follow the group rules!) and join in discussions and sharing of knowledge. Twitter is ablaze with quick reminders, quotes, and viewpoints. Pinterest has beautiful categories and photos as well.

The caveat is, of course, to not lose hours (if not days) to social media. How do you limit your time? It takes a bit of discipline, so decide how long you want to spend on the social media of your choice, and stick to it for at least a week. It may help to schedule a certain amount of time (maybe over your morning coffee or on your public transportation commute) and then move onward with your day.

You can also utilize social media as a tool to encourage others around you. Sharing your positive outlook online can reach those not in your physical vicinity. You can start Facebook groups in which you exchange ideas and practices. You can encourage others to vote, and to take positive action in their life. If photography is your interest, you can encourage others with beautiful photos and images. Do you have an active outdoor life? You could encourage others by example if you post about your wonderful hikes. If you have a certain skill you offer, teach others via Zoom or Facebook Live. Your writing can be shared on all social media platforms and can encourage others with snippets of your personal story or practices. And if you want to be savvier on any of these platforms, there is plenty of information and tutorials to access so you find what fits best for you.

Finding ways to make social media work for you makes it less of a distraction and more of a tool, so in the end you reap the benefits of social media without the time drain that usually accompanies it.

If you find that limiting your time is not doable, then take a break completely. Remove all apps from your phone and try it for a few days at minimum, and at most a week or longer. You can add one app back at a time, very slowly, and see if that helps with the time management of it. Whatever suits you and your life will work best, so take some time to really think about social media's place in your life, how you can manage it, and how you can use it to benefit you.

SPELL BAG

A spell bag is a small cotton bag filled with herbs, crystals, and notes for a specific magical intent. They are useful to keep close to your body, either in a pocket or your bra, to help with the effectiveness of your intention, whether it be love, courage, confidence, or protection. Spell bags can also be created out of small handkerchiefs. Natural materials are best, as they help with the effectiveness of the working.

STATUES

Visual representation of your deity/deities can be a focal point of your altar or your veneration. Statues are made in a variety of materials, so depending on what you find, it could be ceramic, wood, or made of fiber materials. Not only useful for deities, you can also have statues to represent the god/goddess figure, your astrological sign, a cultural symbol, and more. Why is a statue a useful tool for a Positive Pagan? Because they can provide visual interest, remind you of your spirituality, and provide a focal point for meditation. If you create it yourself, it's even more meaningful. Take some time to find a statue that really calls to you, and don't just get one for the sake of getting statuary, because it will just end up being another dusty item on your altar.

TAROT CARDS/ORACLE CARDS

If you decide on tarot or oracle cards, then get a deck and begin. They all come with guidebooks, and it does take continued practice to get used to a deck and its messages. There is an adage that you should always be gifted your first deck, but I don't agree with that. I think it's a beautiful process to pick out your first deck, and whenever possible, do it in person. Much better than ordering it online (if that is your only option however, honor that, and see which decks catch your attention when ordering). I recommend you stand still in front of a selection of tarot cards and observe. Either the artwork or the subject matter will draw your eye, or a deck will literally fall into your hands. I have seen it happen time and time again.

If you order online, make a ritual out of it. Light candles and incense, ground and center yourself, and be open to the selections. Make note of which decks you are drawn to because you may not be drawn to just one! There are so many to choose from that it may take time to select one. When the deck arrives, consecrate it with sacred smoke, incense, or salt. Go through the entire guidebook that comes with it, and carefully look at all the cards individually. What do you notice? Do you like your choice? Does it feel natural in your hands? Do you find the artwork something you will return to again and again?

A great way to learn your divination cards is to pick a card a day and meditate upon its meaning. It can be part of your morning routine, or something you do during the day for a quick break.

Follow the suggestions for spreads in the guidebooks or come up with your own. A spread is a number of cards with a connected meaning. For example, some people pull three cards to represent the past, present, and future.

Positive Pagan Spread

Here is a spread that I like to use:

Get out your favorite tarot or oracle cards.

Shuffle the cards to your satisfaction and then hold them over your heart.

Ask: *What will be for my highest good today?*

Pull three cards. See if a card is catching your eye or sticking out of the deck. Those are usually good ones to pick until you feel comfortable with your intuition.

First card is the message for the day.

Second card is what you should do for others.

Third card is what you can focus on magically in your life.

Enjoy!

Journal Prompt

Time for journaling! List what you consider your favorite tools for Positive Paganism. Any new ones from this list that you wish to add?

The Importance of Deity Worship

As a Pagan, you may already be experiencing a deity or deities as part of your spiritual practice. Or you may consider time in nature as your complete relationship with a deity, taking in nature as a whole entity. How many of us have walked in the woods, sensing something bigger than ourselves? Have you seen faces in trees and mountains? Felt a presence by a babbling brook? Some people dearly want to work with a deity and don't know how to begin. If any of these apply to you, great! The following are suggestions for each aspect of your relationship.

Working with a deity is an important tenet of being a Positive Pagan, and as such, needs to be treated reverently and with care. It is not a relationship to rush into, nor is there a time limit as to when you find or work with a deity. You may work with one or several deities in the course of your practice, and that is perfectly acceptable because it is part of your unique journey.

Working with a deity adds a layer of connection to practices and provides energy and direction to workings and daily life. If the word "deity" is uncomfortable for you, substitute "energy" for the same word. Deities are energies, with their own unique characteristics and purpose. Each one is different, and their place in your life is dependent on you and your personal energy.

As with any earthly relationship, working with a deity involves reciprocity, commitment, care, and respect. If you are already working with a deity (or deities), then you have your own unique story as to how your relationship began. It may have been a dramatic and bold addition to your life, or a quiet, comforting one. There may have been some confusion as to whether any of your contact with a deity was real. You may ask yourself, "Did that really happen? Was I making that up? Am I delusional?"

That moment is common, and you are not alone in thinking those thoughts. How do you know it is real? Quite simply: you do. You will know it is real by what happens during the course of your relationship, little additions to your day, "coincidences" happening, or an unusual effect on your life, such as dreams or happenings that can't be explained. Your relationship with the deities is a journey, so let's explore the variety of ways you can begin, nurture, and maintain that relationship.

BEGINNINGS

How do we begin any relationship or friendship in our life? We have an interest. That person seems interesting or seems to have something in common with you. Have you noticed any deity popping up with regularity in your life? Perhaps articles on Artemis have always caught your attention, or you had a keen interest in Egyptian mythology in school. Maybe Celtic music has always been a favorite, even though you don't have an Irish background. A strong affinity for the ocean might link you to Oya of the African tradition. It takes time and awareness to see the pattern of a deity in your life.

Take some time to really sit with your interest. Write down whatever comes to you as you gaze backward into your life. Is there a yearning for romantic love? Maybe Aphrodite is connected to that longing. Follow up with that interest by researching and reading. Once you delve into the information, notice if you're still interested and want to learn more, or conversely, it doesn't keep your attention.

Be patient with yourself; this is a process. Don't expect to bond with a deity or deities overnight. Possibly, none of them seem of interest to you, and you mostly appreciate being out in nature and feeling that energy. Both answers are correct. The Green Man is often considered the spirit of nature, so if you are comfortable with that, read more about the Green Man, and name that energy the Green Man.

If you don't feel as if you've been able to connect with a deity, then give this meditation a try.

Ritual to Connect with a Deity

Items Needed:

Find a quiet, private space, indoors or outdoors.

White chime candles

An offering of something sweet

Flowers or items from nature (stone, flowers, sticks, nuts, or herbs)

Create a space with a few candles, and an offering of sweets, flowers, or items from nature.

Light the candles.

Play some soothing music quietly in the background if stillness is not preferable for you.

Sit comfortably and close your eyes.

Think of yourself in a large, open field or a favorite spiritual place.

Open your heart and your mind, feel open to receive, and listen.

If you have a deity in mind that you would like to connect with, ask them to join you now. Then begin to speak with the deity, either out loud or inside your head, and talk to them as if they are a friend. Tell them about what's going on in your life, what is bothering you, what joys you have, what you are proud of, and what you need help with, all with no expectation. Take your time in speaking, and make sure you say all that you feel you need to say.

You may get a response in the sense of not feeling quite so alone, or you may not receive any information.

Offer thanks and gratitude for the time spent.

Blow out the candles and spend some time thinking about this experience.

Write in your journal if that helps with processing.

In the coming days and weeks, be more aware of your surroundings. Notice if you have any signs related to what you discussed with your deity, vivid dreams, or interesting happenings. Try this ritual again in a few weeks to build upon your relationship. Tweak this ritual to your own personal needs as you progress in your journey.

Don't get discouraged! Sometimes deities show up in an indirect way, so be open and aware of the process. There are times when we think we are being open, but a layer of skepticism and disbelief exists. It is scary and vulnerable to open yourself up to a deity, so this ritual is a safe and simple way to begin the process. If you feel resistance, then try again another time. Not connecting with a deity is not a reflection of you. It may not be the optimal time in your life for this to happen. Keep it in the back of your mind and go about your life. Trust me, you will know in no uncertain terms if a deity wants to connect with you. Each experience is unique, but you will absolutely know that the deity wanted to make their presence known to you. When that happens, celebrate! It is the beginning of a wonderful relationship.

Meditation to Connect with Your Deity

Sit in a quiet, comfortable position.

Light a candle if that helps you to meditate.

Play soothing music if that helps you be comfortable with the stillness.

Read this section over a few times before you begin this meditation so that you can follow it along without having to memorize anything.

Picture yourself in a forest, walking along a path. Listen to the quiet stillness as you walk, hearing only your footsteps.

Up ahead is a clearing, a wide-open space, with trees surrounding the perimeter.

Walk into the middle of the clearing where you see a circular labyrinth.

Begin your journey in the labyrinth, walking carefully in the winding path.

As you walk toward the middle of the labyrinth, you notice a large stone, marking its place. Stop at this stone and take a few deep breaths.

Bending down carefully, trace the edges of this stone. Feel the warm, slightly rough edges, and then lift it up.

Underneath the stone is a hole. A sweet, grassy smell rushes up from the opening.

Take a deep breath and jump into the hole.

You are safe.

It is a tunnel that you fall down, with the wind rushing past you. But it's not scary. You land at the bottom on a large, welcoming cushion. You get up and walk forward. The passageway leads to a door. What is behind the door?

The rest of the journey is up to you!

What is behind the door?

Is there an object there for you to take back with you?

Do you sense a presence behind the door?

What kind of energy does this presence have?

Take this journey and see where it takes you. When you are complete and satisfied with what happens, return to the path where you began, and come back to the present moment. What did you see? What made an impression on you? Jot down a few notes in your journal. Let the experience settle into your system and see if you come up with any insights. It may not happen right away, so be patient and kind with yourself.

Try this journey a few times, and if it is a comfortable way to connect with your deity, then do so again, as often as you'd like. Tweak the experience to what feels comfortable for you.

INTUITION

Identifying your intuition, or your "gut feeling," comes from practice and stillness. If you're not sure how to identify your intuition, think about a time where a thought crossed your mind and it came to pass. That's one basic example. For some, it is akin to a soft, still voice that guides. Your intuition will thrive in stillness. Meditation is ideal, but if you're not fond of meditation, then sitting quietly will also do. Make time in the morning or evening, and in the stillness notice what thoughts cross your mind. If there are situations where things can go in one of two directions, then sit in the stillness and see which choice resonates with you more.

Another way to note your intuition is to observe how your body reacts. The brain can tell you different stories, but the body does not. Know how you get butterflies when you are anxious about things, or your body tenses up in a situation that seems harmless.

Some people use divination to bring forth answers, guided by intuition. Using cards or pendulums will assist in this process.

BE AUTHENTIC

When working with deities, it is important that you're comfortable with being authentic. Being authentic means your actions and words reflect the person you are, not the person you think you should be. As with intention, authenticity is an important touchstone in your work with deities. Knowing what you believe in and who you are as a person is part of the journey and relationship with the deities. If you are not sure who you are, take time to get to really know yourself. It helps to begin with lists. Write down what you like about yourself, and then a list of attributes you're not fond of, and keep discerning what is true and authentic in those lists. Be sure to write down how you truly feel, not a story you've told yourself or what you've been told throughout your life.

It takes time to sort through messages you've received about yourself when you're attempting to be your most authentic self. If you have been told you're a failure, then success feels like a far-away or impossible prize. Take the focus off the negative aspects about yourself and begin with the positive attributes you have. For example, if you have been told you're a failure or a screwup, then list what you're good at in life. List everything, from giving good hugs, to being a creative cook, to someone who is always there for their friends. List things you truly like about yourself; no detail is too small to notice. When you meditate or have quiet time, focus on that list. Post it where you can see it, and list it in your head so you can recite it, almost like a poem.

Get used to being nice to yourself. This may seem like an odd thing to do or think about, but sometimes being nice to yourself is the last thing you'd think of doing. Do you speak harshly to yourself? Would you talk to a close friend like that? Monitor your inner conversations, and if you notice a lot of negative words and phrases popping up, try to substitute a positive attribute instead. Saying you are protecting your physical energy is a lot more gentle than lazy.

Once you are comfortable in your own skin, then examine how you present yourself to the world. Are you negative, dismissive, or self-absorbed? Examine yourself closely or ask friends how you come across. Work on things you can change with small steps so it doesn't feel overwhelming. Say one positive thing a day, show interest in a friend's new endeavor, and pause to think about what you're going to say before speaking.

Self-examination can be challenging but is well worth the effort. The more authentic you are, the easier it will be to connect with the deities. Who wouldn't want to communicate with your most authentic self?

CONNECT

The next step is to connect with the deity. I recommend connecting with one deity at a time so you can be clear about your lines of communication. Sometimes deities work in tandem, and some prefer individual attention. You will learn about the preference as your relationship deepens.

To connect with a deity, set aside some time to really devote to this action. In front of your altar is a great place to begin, but it can also happen outside, in your bedroom, or even your office. The important thing is that you are comfortable and open to the experience.

Light a candle or several. White candles are easiest to attain, and also denote purity. You are at the beginning of your relationship, so no need to invest in different colors or intentions.

Prepare an offering. Until you know the deity's preferences, no need to be elaborate. A cup of wine, a glass of water or whiskey, or whatever you have on hand will be fine. Even a cup of tea or coffee is acceptable. Add fruit or a small cake if possible. As with human friendships, you want to be hospitable!

Once you prepare the sacred space with the candles and offerings, set a quiet intention of connection with the deity. If it helps to have soothing music in the background, please do so.

Then, talk to them.

Yes, as if you were talking to a friend. Tell them about yourself and about your interest in them. It can be out loud or in your head, but be authentic. If there is something you want help with, then include that, and why you need help. Be careful not to list a series of wants like a Christmas list. Be genuine about what you desire. It could be unblocking creativity, a new job or relationship, or anything you've been feeling stuck with in your life. Offer gratitude that you learned about them, and the possibility of connection. You can also ask for a sign that you are heard, and that they want to work with you. Be excited about future interactions.

At this point, it is helpful to be still, and listen.

You may have phrases or mental visions pop up, but if not, don't be concerned. When you are done, snuff out the candle.

If possible, leave the altar as is, but if you need to move it, then do so at this point.

Notice your dreams as you sleep that evening. They may be more vivid or present a clue that your deity is responding to you.

If you don't remember your dreams, be aware of your surroundings and notice any little sign that may be from your deity. You may start seeing hearts in many places if you are reaching out to Aphrodite, or oak leaves as a nod to Brigid, showing up more in daily walks.

Once you feel you've received a sign, offer thanks to your deity and include spending time at your altar as part of your daily routine.

If you feel that nothing is happening, don't be disheartened. Repeat this process with the deity for a few months and see what happens. Follow the steps above.

Once you have given it your efforts, and months have passed, don't be discouraged. It may not be time to connect with that particular deity.

Follow this process with any deity and be open to the possibilities. Make sure you choose thoughtfully and with conviction because superficial interest or self-absorption will not result in a response.

HONORING YOUR DEITIES

Pagans often use the words "working with" or "honoring" their deity / deities, as it is very much a reciprocal relationship, as previously mentioned.

Deities show up in unexpected ways, so you may not notice their gentle nudges until it is a major push, or they will call you so clearly you might feel bewildered. As in a love relationship, when you know, you know. Working with a deity is listening to them, following their requests and lead, as well as honoring them. Relationships with them are as varied; some may last a season, some may ask for your undivided loyalty, and some work in tandem with others, receding or moving to the foreground as needed. Being a Positive Pagan is boosted by your relationship with your deities because it feels like they have your back, support you, are there for you, and their energy is a boost.

Taking time out of your morning to honor your deities is an investment in your relationship with them. It doesn't need to take a lot of time; a quick visit to your altar to make an offering or verbally checking in are good ways to keep the lines of communication open. If you don't have time in the morning, you can certainly do this in the evening, and possibly spend more time if it works with your schedule.

Another way to honor your deities is to learn about them. Research their history, stories, favorite colors, preferred offerings, and more. The deities appreciate the effort you put in and adding to your knowledge will help you to know them better. There is so much information out there, both online and in books. You may find things you have in common; note what seems familiar about them to you if you do.

Spending time with them in silence is also welcome. Sit in front of your altar and focus on your deity. If you don't have an altar, you can sit with a book about them, or in front of a candle and a picture of them. Sit in silence and listen. Do not get frustrated if you don't hear anything at first. There are times when it feels like you're talking into a void. Some of the best advice I've ever received was to speak to deities as if they were your friend. Pour your heart out to them, and tell them what's going on, what you're missing, and what is needed. Not in a complaining tone, but as you would tell a friend who asks, "How are you doing?" The deities want to know what's in your heart. Know that you are being listened to and have faith that answers will come.

Candles are also a wonderful way to honor your deity. Plain candles are fine, but if you are feeling creative, you can create a seven-day candle devoted to your deity. You can find plain seven-day candles in grocery and metaphysical stores.

Before you begin, look up the correspondences for your deity. It is as easy as googling "(Your deity name) correspondence herbs and candles" and information related to all sorts of things related to your deity will pop up.

Deity Altar

Setting up a deity altar is pretty straightforward. Find a small table or space and cover it with an altar cloth. Using a color that is associated with your deity would be lovely, but whatever you use is suitable. Place candles, statues, and offerings related to your deity on top of the cloth. Change up the offerings as you are moved to, including portions of celebratory meals and drinks on occasion.

Seven-Day Deity Candle

Items Needed:

One seven-day candle (choose a color related to your deity, but if you are not sure, plain white will work)

Artwork related to your deity (the easiest is to print
off the internet, or to make it even more personal,
use your own drawings and art)
1 Tsp oil (olive, almond, sunflower)
Herbs related to your deity (if you're not sure, it's
okay to use what you have on hand)

Decorate your candle with the artwork you have chosen. If you would like to leave it plain, that's fine as well.

Dip your finger into the oil and anoint the top of the candle until it is covered.

Take a small pinch of the herbs and place on top of the oil.

Before you light the candle, set your intention. It can be simple, as in hope for a peaceful day, or beginning your relationship with your deity.

Gaze into the flame. Notice if any thoughts or images pop up.

When done, snuff out the candle.

As a rule of thumb, if you snuff out the candle, the work and intention you set will continue. If you blow it out with your breath, then the work and intention ends, and you will need to start over the next time you light the candle.

Also, you can skip these steps and find a candle already dressed and intended for your deity online, such as Etsy. I highly recommend Etsy for finding what you need for your spiritual practice if you don't have the time and inclination to make something yourself. Plus, you will be supporting our artistic Pagan community, so it's a very Positive Pagan thing to do.

One of the other items I like to create to honor my deity is a Deity Offering Bag. It's fairly simple, and it changes with the seasons or celebrations on the Wheel of the Year.

Deity Offering Bag

Try to have this ready by the Full Moon, which is great for charging.

Items Needed:

Small cloth bag (either a small cotton or mesh bag used for jewelry, even a small cloth handkerchief is great)

Herbs and crystals associated with your deity (you can look this up, or if you feel called to create a bag filled with local nature items, do that instead)

Twine or ribbon

Fill your cloth bag with your items and tie it so the contents don't fall out.

Charge it on your altar under a Full Moon. If you can't wait, leaving it on your deity altar can also charge it, and then you can add the boost of a Full Moon charge the next time it rolls around.

I usually leave the bag on the altar, but if I set an intention and go into a situation where I need an extra boost, I will take it with me. I also take Deity Offering Bags on road trips or leave them in the car if I am doing a lot of driving. It functions as both a protective measure and a portable deity altar when I keep it in the car.

A Deity Offering Bag can also be left at a nature spot where you feel particularly attuned, but only do this if the ingredients are 100 percent biodegradable. I've often left items at the base of a favorite tree for my deity: a small pile of herbs and a tiny pour of whiskey onto the ground. I've also poured plant-based milks as an offering, and left a few items gathered on my nature walk. In my experience, the deities appreciate when we honor them, and the positive energy you put toward these actions reflects back to you so you feel good when doing so.

OTHER WAYS TO HONOR YOUR DEITY

Acts of charity and financial contributions work to honor your deity. (A cause close to your deity's association would be lovely. If your deity is associated with the literary arts, you can donate to a local writing group or bring them treats you've baked yourself. The possibilities are endless.)

Spending time with your deity. If you can only spend a few minutes at your altar at the most, then carve out an hour or so when you are free to spend time with your deity. Light a candle and bring fresh flowers or offerings to their altar, talk to them, or read about them.

Create! If you knit, embroider, crochet, sew, paint, or love working with miniatures, use these skills to create an item for your deity. It can be a new altar cloth, a painting, or a small tableau of items related to your deity.

Journal about your relationship with your deity. Make note of different items you have placed on the altar, different intentions you set, messages you received, and prayers or chants that you create.

Another way to honor them is to use prayer beads when you spend time at their altar or sacred space. Each bead can be one of their attributes, and you can incorporate it into prayer or meditation. For example, *I honor your strength, your wisdom, and your tenacity (three beads). May I feel strength, wisdom, and tenacity in the coming days (three more beads).*

Prayer beads help focus your attention on areas you want to build upon, or it can be a list of what you are grateful for in your life, if you are unsure what to say. Some people may be uncomfortable with the word "prayer," so you can also use the beads for setting intentions.

Journaling is also a lovely way to interact with your deity. For some, writing is easier than speaking, so if you prefer to pour your heart out to your deity in a journal, please do so. Purchase a notebook specifically for the purpose and set the intention to write a certain amount of time each week. It can be in the form of a letter, lists, or a combination of information that you have learned about the deity, along with your thought processes. Keeping this journal in the sacred space or altar you set aside for them is a lovely gesture of connection.

You can also acknowledge your deity with statues or jewelry that represent them, or if you're feeling creative, you can paint a representation of them to add to your altar. If you are a writer, dedicate a poem or blessings written in their honor.

Honoring your deity with a meal is also a wonderful way to connect with your deity. If they have a certain celebration or day attached to them (for example, Imbolc for Brigid), prepare foods and drinks pertaining to that celebration. Set a place for them at the table if you'd like. There are many wonderful Pagan cookbooks and Sabbat celebration books that are full of ideas you can incorporate.

Some of the happiest and most Positive Pagans I know have deep and meaningful relationships with their deities, and their lives reflect their devotion. There is a serene calmness in knowing you are not alone, and that some powerful deities are watching out for you. Honor them morning or night, but be sure to take at least part of your day in community with them.

HONORING NATURE AS YOUR DEITY

If no specific deity holds an appeal for you and you feel that nature itself is your deity, then honor nature by doing the following:

- Tend to a favorite nature spot, keeping it free from litter.
- Carry all your trash with you when hiking and dispose and recycle when you get home.

- Leave birdseed out for birds and nuts out for squirrels.

- Observe the wildlife in your area.

- Contribute to conservation efforts.

- Learn more about the aspects of nature that fascinate you: birding, plant life, or tree identification.

- Download a naturalist app (I recommend Seek) and learn to identify plants in your area.

- Take part in efforts to keep local water clean.

- If you live in a city, set up a small herb garden on your windowsill. Let that be your way to honor nature.

- Go to a local park and help keep it clean.

Journal Prompt

Which deities have you been drawn to, and which one(s) do you feel like you have a relationship with now? What characteristics of the deities are you drawn to? What signs or interactions have you noticed happening recently? Which of the suggestions in this chapter spoke to you and why?

CHAPTER

4

Cleansing Your Surroundings

Your surroundings are the canvas of your life. If you view your life as a piece of art, it changes your perspective. What to add? What to get rid of? Is it ever complete? As with any work of art, you are the artist and in control. Outside forces can buffet your world, but you are the one in charge of working on that painting. You may collaborate with others, but ultimately, you sign your name in the corner and create your masterpiece.

Your surroundings are your art, and it impacts your ability to recharge and renew so you can maintain your positivity. Each day is a renewal and a chance to create magic, so to do that, surround yourself with things filled with a sense of ease and flow. Remaining positive in this decidedly offbeat world is work, and a daily choice. What makes that choice a little easier is having conducive surroundings to help you make positive choices that enhance your life.

TAKE A LOOK AROUND

So, let us begin. Put this book down for a moment and take a look at your surroundings. What is your home space like? Is it cluttered and crowded or minimalist and serene? Is it a reflection of who you are, or are there piles of possessions everywhere? Is there something you would like to change, or too many changes to ponder?

Looking at the big picture can be overwhelming, so focus on one area you can change easily. Today. Yes, clearing a small corner of space can help boost your mood, and you will have accomplished something. Action is recommended as a go-to plan for when feeling downcast or unmotivated, so even something as small as clearing out one drawer or shelf can help boost mood levels.

The goal is to have your space and surroundings feel good to you, so that you can, in turn, truly embody a Positive Pagan. It does require a bit of self-examination and knowing what you like. Do you like the minimalist look, or do you prefer cozy belongings throughout the room? What would reflect you as a person?

To begin, sit down with a mug of your favorite beverage and look around your space. Is it possible to create a vision of what you want your surroundings to look like? Would it look completely different, or does it just need a few tweaks?

Is there space for you to conduct your spiritual practices?

Is your bedroom a restful space?

Positive Pagan Space Ritual

Try this ritual to help you narrow down your focus.

Items Needed:

Paper

Writing instrument

Rose quartz

Garnet

Plant or vase of wildflowers

Sit down at a table with some paper and your writing instrument. Take a few deep breaths, holding your rose quartz and garnet. Gaze at the plant or wildflowers and take a moment to appreciate their beauty. Close or lower your eyes. Visualize a bare space and then slowly fill it with items that make you feel happy and serene. Plants, furniture, art on the walls. Once you have that visual, open your eyes and write on one side of the paper how you felt in that space. On the other side of the paper write all the words that describe the space in its entirety: colors, scents, style, items, descriptors, such as light, dark, etc. When done, look over the lists and circle anything that is repeated. Place stars next to what feels doable in the near future. Keep that visual in mind as you create and change your space in the coming weeks and months. Fold up the list, keep it on your altar, and place the crystals upon it. Refer back to the list as needed.

POSITIVE PAGAN CHECKLIST

That ritual was to help prepare your mindset for your surroundings. It should flow from here into action as you move throughout your space, noting what changes are needed (if any).

We are going to go through basic spaces of a home, along with other areas that you spend time in (car, office, etc.) using the following checklist:

- Declutter

- Cleanse (physically and spiritually)

- Draw out the vibrancy

- Protection

It's nearly impossible to be consistently positive if you are in a world of chaos in your home. If you are in a situation where you can't find a personal quiet space, or if there is not an option to clear out clutter, start with at least one thing. Let's begin with one simple space, the heart of your spiritual practice: your altar.

REFRESHING YOUR ALTAR

Your altar is central to your spiritual practice. If you want to have a daily spiritual practice, or if you did, and this has fallen to the way-side, I recommend bringing your focus to your altar.

Declutter Do you have a space for an altar? Is it a table or a shelf filled with clutter? Or is it a representation of who you are, the deities you honor, and the practice you hold? Do you have more than one altar? If it is a bit of a mess right now, take a deep breath. This one is easy to remedy! Take everything off your main altar (if you have more than one), put it to one side, and look at it with fresh eyes. Ask yourself the following questions: What would you like your altar focus to be? Do you want to honor all your deities or just one? Would you prefer to have a theme (seasons, holidays, Wheel of the Year) or have all natural items on it?

Cleanse Cleanse with water, salt, and smoke. Dust thoroughly, then use moon, spring, or Florida Water to clean the area, and change the energy with smoke. Use incense or burn herbs on a charcoal disc in your cauldron or a fireproof dish, along with cleansing herbs such as bay leaves, rosemary, or lavender.

Draw Out the Vibrancy Select objects for your altar that reflect you and what resonates with you. Choose with care, and if you're not exactly sure what you want, start simply with a candle and one object. This spot will provide you peace and focus, so which objects reflect that for you?

Protection Simple is best, so a small bowl of natural salt with protective herbs such as juniper, mugwort, or rosemary work well.

YOUR BED

The most useful suggestion I can give about your home is this: *make your bed*. I know. It seems too simple, right? Making your bed is not only a positive action, but you have also accomplished one thing to start your day. Our world tends to revolve around accomplishments and getting things done, and yes, you can spend entire days doing nothing. But making the bed is such a declarative action. It's a good feeling while doing it, and it feels soothing when you go to bed at night. The sight of a made bed is much better than climbing over the chaos of an unmade bed. Don't believe me? Try it for a week and see if it makes a difference in how you feel.

We are in our beds for at least a few hours each twenty-four-hour period, so why not make it pleasant? Use sheets that feel good against your skin, pillows that cradle your head, a nightstand with books, a soothing light, some crystals, a candle or two, and artwork or plants that make you smile. Often that bedside table becomes a catchall, so take some time to strip it down and start over with just a few items. Another thing is then accomplished!

THE BEDROOM

The bedroom should be your sanctuary. If it has to double as an office or ritual space, make sure those areas are clearly designated. It helps keep the energy clear for what you need to do and where.

Have some art in your room, something lovely to gaze at. If it's in your eye's view when you awake, so much the better.

Hang wind chimes or create a mobile in honor of your deity or deities. This can include beautiful items from nature, Pagan symbols (triquetra, pentacle, stars, moons, etc.), bells, or pictures.

Drape twinkle lights over your headboard or altar area for soft lighting.

Use candles for decor and altar use where you can. Buy inexpensive, plain seven-day candles at the dollar or grocery store and decorate them with stickers or artwork printed out. I usually create a red Brigid seven-day candle near every Imbolc, decorated with different artwork that represents her, along with pictures of items she is associated with, such as poetry books, beer, blacksmithing, and fire. It's a fun and inexpensive way of honoring her, and more personal than a purchased one.

Your nightstand is an important part of your bedroom. It's not just a depository, although it can sometimes end up that way. Just like all other spaces, clear it off, clean it, and be selective what stays. Rugs are important, no matter the size of the room. A small rug in front of your bed is a great place to get dressed, to warm your feet on a winter's day, or to brighten up the room.

This is the room where you spend time sleeping, so try to keep it as peaceful and as positive as possible. If you have a bed, a place for your clothes, and a few inexpensive tables, the rest can be books, plants, art, or whatever makes you feel good. Make sure it's a restful place, and not a landscape of piles everywhere. As a Positive Pagan, I find it useful to not be weighed down with *stuff*, so try to lighten your load whenever you can.

Declutter Clothes and other items can clutter up the bedroom more than anything else, so make it a habit to do a clean sweep of the extra items you have around and put things away. If you are in a small space where storage is at a premium, try keeping only what is necessary in your bedroom, and either put the extra in another part of your home, or donate items. A quick way to go through items gauging its use: are you using this item, hoping to use it, or does it have sentimental value? If everything was cleared out of your home in one click of your fingers, what would you keep?

Cleanse Sprinkling Florida Water in all four corners of your bedroom is a great way to keep the energy clear. Try doing it every other month and notice the difference. If you don't want to use liquid, you can also use natural salt. Sprinkle some in all four corners of the room, but let it stay there for a few days to absorb any negative energy. Sweep it away and enjoy the bonus of sweeping your bedroom floor along with the salt.

Draw Out the Vibrancy Light will draw out the vibrancy in your room, so bring out the light in any way that you can: brighter colors, candles, colorful bedding, or decorative tapestries on the wall. Along with the cleansing, make sure the energy in your bedroom remains light and your sleep will benefit from it.

Protection For an easy protection method, place a bowl of natural salt under your bed, or a large piece of tourmaline. The added benefit of tourmaline is that it is a grounding stone, helping to redirect negative energy into positive. It's great for more restful sleep.

FRONT DOOR

Do you use your front door, a side door, or do you come into your home from the garage? Whichever entry door you use, it's worth clearing the energy from it regularly. Try to do this on the first or last day of each month. Think about this: if you live in an apartment, the energy out in the hallway is a collection of all your neighbors' energy, and whoever comes through the door of your space is bringing their own energy into your home. Even if you keep your visitors to a minimum, your door is a portal to you, so keep that entry cleansed and protected.

A good way to provide a positive threshold into your space is to create a ward of positivity and protection so that those who cross your doorway feel uplifted.

Positivity Ward Ritual

Items Needed:

An 8-oz. Mason jar with lid

Natural salt

Lemon peel from 3 lemons (or 15 drops of lemon essential oil)

2 cinnamon sticks

2–3 small citrine or sodalite stones

4 pennies

In the Mason jar, layer the salt and lemon peel (or essential oil), insert the cinnamon sticks and stones, and then fill the rest of the jar with salt. Add the pennies. Cover securely with the lid, shake so all the materials mix in the jar, and keep it in a dark cabinet for 9 days.

When you open the jar, fish out the pennies with a metal or wooden spoon (don't use your fingers, as it will disturb the energy contained in the working). Place the pennies outside the four corners of your home (if you live in an apartment, indoor corners are fine if you can't place the pennies on the four corners outside).

As you place the pennies, envision a protective, sunny barrier arising from the pennies, filled with positivity, protection, safety, and care. Look up and envision the barriers forming a roof over your home. This warding will be good for a season, so be sure to refresh at the beginning of each new season, repeating the steps above.

The salt can be used on the threshold of your home. Sprinkle a handful of salt on the doorstep and let it settle for a few hours (if possible) to absorb any negativity or chaotic energy. Sweep up and discard the salt. All who cross your threshold will step through a barrier of positivity and serenity.

Declutter If your entryway is filled with lots of shoes, coats, or other items, take some time to clean it up and minimize the number of items in the area. Clear the area so that energy can flow more freely into your space, hopefully bringing with it all you'd like to flow into your home: abundance, love, and joy.

Cleanse To cleanse the front door, use this homemade Home Cleansing Spray. Not only is it good for cleaning, but it also leaves a pleasant, welcoming smell when used.

Homemade Cleansing Spray
Items Needed:
16-oz. Mason jar
Lemon peels from 3 lemons
White vinegar
3 sprigs of rosemary
Glass spray bottle

Place the lemon peels in the Mason jar and cover with white vinegar. Add the rosemary sprigs, cover, and leave in a dark place for 2 weeks. Strain and add the mixture to the spray bottle. Label as Cleansing Spray and use when needed.

Draw Out the Vibrancy Doorways are such magical places, as they provide entry between one space to the next. It is a liminal space in our home, and most of the time we don't pay attention. Stand in your doorway and look outward and back inward. Note if what you see is pleasing to the eye. Need a plant by the front door? A welcoming wreath of herbs or a string of bells on the door? Looking inward, would a mat be useful for clearing off shoe dirt? Is there a place for shoes to be placed? Try keeping shoes off throughout your home, as it cuts down on cleaning, and also keeps whatever you've picked up on your shoes (dirt, energy, sticky substances) by the door. Also, keep a tray by the door to drop your keys, wallet, and purse so they're always reliably found in one spot. This cuts down on searches for these items when you get into the habit of leaving them by the door.

Protection A permanent sign of protection over your door is an added boost, whether it is a horseshoe or horse brass. (Horse brass are decorative plaques made of brass that were used to decorate horse harnesses and are nowadays used magically for protection and luck.) Is there a symbol representing protection in your family culture? Evil eye? Hamsa? Brigid's Wheel? Perhaps you can create your own sigil of protection or have a small bowl of sacred water (moon water or water you've imbued with protection magic and herbs such as cloves, rosemary, and sage) by the door that you can dip your fingers in as you arrive and depart.

YOUR CAR

It is a good practice to get your shields up and your protection in place each time you get into your car. Hang an item from your rearview mirror, which can also be used as a reminder to ground and shield before you depart on your trip. (Be sure to check with your local laws before hanging something in your car.) The item can be a symbol of protection, a hagstone, or a strip of cloth into which you have spoken words of protection and intention of safe travel.

Vehicle Protection Ritual

Items Needed:

Florida Water

Sacred smoke of your choosing

*Item of protection (either crystals, a hematite piece
    of jewelry, or whatever works as a protective
    crystal for you. Listen to your intuition as to
    what to use for your item of protection. It could
    be an item from someone who has passed on who
    you feel still protects you. Be creative and really
    listen to what resonates.)*

Ground and shield yourself, taking deep breaths as you begin this ritual.

Call in your ancestors and guardians in the four directions as you circle the car.

Place your hand on the car and send it gratitude for getting you safely to destinations, and for all its help for your transportation needs.

If guided, walk around the car, drawing personal sigils of protection or a pentacle with the smoke, especially over all window spaces.

Sprinkle Florida Water on the floor in front of all the seats. Sprinkle a small amount along the dashboard, being careful not to get the Florida Water into anything mechanical.

Add your item of protection by attaching it to the rearview mirror or putting in the glovebox or wherever you feel it is best placed. Under the driver's seat is also a good location but think about whether or not you'd prefer to have it in your view when you drive.

Now open the circle, thanking and releasing your guardians and ancestors in the four directions.

This is a good ritual to do at least once a year and after any major work that has been done to the car. Cars are not indestructible, so things break down and repairs are needed from time to time. In my experience, regularly sending your car some positive energy and love is as vital as checking the tires and your oil.

Consider naming your car or at least referring to it affectionately as a bonus boost, as it can only help add to the positivity surrounding your mode of transportation! Please note that this ritual can also be adapted to most other modes of transportation, so adjust as needed.

Declutter Keep your car free of clutter and try not to get into the habit of throwing mail or fast-food trash in the back. If items pile up because life gets busy, make a note to clean it out when you have time, and follow it up with some cleansing.

Cleanse Cleanse your car with Florida Water or the cleansing spray used with your front door. You can also cleanse via smoke using incense.

Draw Out the Vibrancy If your car is your main source of transportation, you are probably already taking good care of it with regularly scheduled maintenance and periodic cleaning. Adding some magic via crystals and cleansing will also help boost the vibrancy. Expanding the magic to your passengers by placing a protective crystal under the passenger seat will also add to your car's vibrancy. Clear the energy in your car by going for a drive with the windows down on a warm day and playing upbeat music. Notice how different it feels when you do, and then make it a regular habit.

Protection When washing your car, add a few drops of Florida Water or cleansing spray. Say words of intention of safety and safe travel as you wash the body of the car, as well as when you clean the interior.

THE KITCHEN

The kitchen is the heart and hearth of the home, and sometimes it becomes a magnet for clutter and barely functional. For Positive Pagans, this room is where we gain energy and sustenance to face the world. To gain a sense of ease, begin with clearing out cabinets, donating extra food items (check the expiration date, please!), and getting rid of excess Tupperware.

A good rule of thumb is to keep things as natural as possible, so try to rid your kitchen of plasticware whenever you can. Collect glass jars to keep extra spices or leftovers in or use them as vases. Try to have natural utensils, cloth napkins and kitchen towels. Simple and sturdy cookware and whatever utensils you need can be easy to find in thrift shops and Goodwill. As with any other project, don't think you have to overhaul everything at once, unless you're one of those rare people who enjoy that! Follow your energy level and see where it takes you. Maybe one utensil drawer, for today, and organize your spice cabinet next week.

An addition to your kitchen might be adding a kitchen altar. Not much space is needed for one. Some people like to put a kitchen altar on the counter, and some like to use a window sill, or a small space near the sink. What's on it is up to you; it can include spices, a salt bowl, or a cup of water with some fresh herbs in it. Perhaps a statue of your favorite deity, or a photograph of an ancestor who was known to be a good cook. Other useful items such as a mortar and pestle (nothing like grinding away your aggressions on some spices!), a small candle, and an offering bowl are plenty. Kitchen altars can add magic to the mundane task of cooking and can provide a visual reminder of that as you prepare food.

The energy of the kitchen is very powerful. It is the place where we create food, nourishment, comfort, welcome, and it can also be a respite. Some kitchens can be cluttered, messy, and a bit sad. Try observing yours with an objective eye to see what you can brighten up.

If your kitchen is small, do not despair! Look online for organization tips and get yourself to a store that specializes in storage items. When the kitchen is to your satisfaction, be sure to cleanse the energy in the kitchen. Use sacred smoke, herbs grown from your garden, or Florida Water. A salt bowl is also useful for absorbing any negative energy. Be sure to refresh it when needed.

Salt Bowls

Items Needed:

Ceramic bowl (thrift stores are a great place to find these)

Natural salt (for example, sea salt or Himalayan salt)

Additional herbs (Rosemary, juniper, and thyme are good ones)

Tealight

Place the salt in a ceramic bowl. Let your intuition guide you as to which herbs to use. It's always fun to see which herbs call to you. Then look up their magical properties, either in books or online. You may surprise yourself with how on point your intuition is!

Place the tealight on top of the salt.

Light the tealight.

Notice the energy change. It's always an amazing feeling!

Added bonus: Throw the windows open and air out the kitchen as well. Notice the freshness and offer a few moments of gratitude to your deity or deities.

Declutter Consider decluttering not only kitchen items, but food items. Simplify your food choices to start with and get rid of the excess. Do you have a friend who is an amazing cook? Give that person the exotic, expensive spice you used for one dish and haven't touched since. Use whole foods as much as possible and try to decrease the amount of processed food in your diet. A simple wooden bowl of apples is much more pleasing to the eye and palate than ten boxes of sugary cereals in a row. No judgement, but make a point not to purchase any more, and get back to simple, healthy breakfasts, lunches, dinners, and snacks. Try to eliminate sugar from your diet as well to detox your body from it. There are plenty of natural alternatives. If you have piles of cookbooks, get rid of the ones you don't use regularly and put them in a bookcase or donate them. Or recycle them as gifts.

Cleanse There is a fine line between cozy clutter and chaos in a kitchen. Take a good long look and see where your line is: more cozy or chaotic? Look at your kitchen with fresh eyes and get it to a manageable state. When you clean your kitchen, add an extra boost by stirring the sudsy water a magical number of times (3, 6, 9) and speak words of intention as you wipe down floors, counters, and cabinets. As with the other rooms, a good sprinkling of Florida Water or sacred water in the corners every quarter will also give you a boost.

Draw Out the Vibrancy How to make your kitchen more vibrant? If you don't have a fireplace, which is usually considered the hearth of the home, then create a mini hearth in your kitchen. Place candles on a tray and light them when you want to draw in positive energy and center yourself. Gazing into candles has always been a soothing activity, so make some time in your schedule to do this, especially when the world feels topsy-turvy.

Protection Make or buy a kitchen witch! A kitchen witch is a homemade doll that resembles a stereotypical witch. Google "kitchen witch" for ideas and create one with items you have around your home. Get creative or purchase one. A kitchen witch historically has been used to ward off negative spirits and is considered a good luck charm in many European countries.

THE OFFICE

If you have an office in your home, keep all your work items in it and try not to let them migrate throughout the rest of your home. That is a physical boundary you can set, and a choice you make so work stays where you work. A designated work area can be a magical space, so think of how you can boost your space magically.

Crystals are the easiest and simplest way to boost magic in your work space. Some work crystals to consider include tourmaline for protection, dumortierite for patience, citrine for positive energy, rose quartz for love, and carnelian for creativity. You can have a few crystals in a pretty bowl near your work space to use them as touchstones during the day or as a visual break if you have lots of computer work to do. It is also useful to have divination tools nearby to use for a quick reading on a situation. Lit candles are good for stress relief or relaxation, and an oil diffuser can be a lovely, scented addition.

One final note: get a prosperity bill to add to your office, as it's especially useful toward bringing in abundance. A prosperity bill is similar to paper money, but it is coated in gold, and obviously fake. They also make great gifts! Drawing in abundance can be in the form of money, projects, clients, or whatever relates to the work you do. Keep your Gratitude Journal or Gratitude Jar nearby because it helps throughout the day, when you get stressed or anxious about work, to take a moment to write down a few things you're grateful for, whether it be a client interaction, new work, or satisfaction with a job well done. If you can have a statue or picture of your deity or deities nearby, all the better. It helps with feeling isolated while you work.

Declutter Keep your workspace as organized as you can or make plans to tidy it up at the end of your work week. It takes a few minutes and can help cut down on frantic searches for misplaced items. Throw out old pens, take out the garbage, and recycle your papers.

Cleanse If you use an oil diffuser, consider using a mint oil for mental clarity and cleansing purposes. Or have a small vase with fresh herbs, such as mint or lavender. Consider a sage or rose water spray for a quick boost.

Rose Water Office Cleanse Spray

Items Needed:

4–5 roses (organic and natural is best)

A pot with a lid

Small bowl

Spring or filtered water

Ice cubes

Glass spray bottle

1 sprig of rosemary

Remove the petals from the roses, brushing off any dirt or little bugs you may encounter. Place the petals in a pot with the bowl nestled in the middle of it. Cover the roses with the water (but keep the small bowl clear of any water or rose petals, as it will catch the distillation of the rose water). Place the pot on the stove and place the lid upside down on the pot. As the pot heats up, add the ice to the upside-down lid, as this helps with the condensation process. Add more ice as it melts. After about 30–40 minutes, there should be enough rose water in the bowl contained in the pot to fill a small spray bottle with rose water. Add the sprig of rosemary and use as needed. Add the wilted petals to your compost or take them outside as an offering.

Draw Out the Vibrancy What would make your workspace more vibrant? A plant or a vase of flowers? Do you have items that reflect you within the space, or is it all work? If your work is your passion, display items that reflect your industry and what you appreciate most about it. Would you prefer reminders of your magical life in your workspace? Designate a small area with your items, such as tarot/oracle cards, some crystals, a candle, and a small piece of magical art.

Protection Refresh your protection at least weekly, if not daily. Other people's energies can be picked up during your interactions, so be vigilant about grounding and shielding. A piece of tourmaline nearby should be enough to help when this happens. Wash your hands, hold the tourmaline, and set the intention of clearing the energy. When done, wash your hands again so the negativity washes away.

THE BATHROOM

If you have a tub, you have a ritual space! Make it beautiful with a few candles and maybe some decorative soaps. Keep your tub clean, making sure to get to all the nooks and crannies where dust can gather.

Cleansing baths are a necessary part of a Positive Pagan's life for many reasons: to clear the spiritual muck off yourself, to prepare yourself for a sacred space and ritual, and as an act of self-love. This can also be done in the shower, although the process is a bit different.

Positive Pagan Bath Ritual

Items Needed:

A few handfuls of natural salt

A few drops of apple cider vinegar

A can or bottle of beer (doesn't matter which kind, inexpensive is fine)

Epsom salts

Natural herbs (Research which herbs you will need for your specific purpose. For example, mugwort is good for calming and has antibacterial properties. Place the herbs in a tea strainer or small cloth bag so your tub doesn't fill with small pieces of herbs. Or not, whichever you prefer.)

Lavender essential oil

Remember to use warm water, not hot. Focus on the purpose of the bath as you prepare and add all items. Light candles, play soothing music, and take several deep breaths as you soak in the water.

Bathe, and when done, be sure to rinse yourself with fresh water as the tub drains, releasing all that no longer serves or is needed by you.

Showers are wonderful for releasing negativity, along with the water cascading down the drain.

This ritual is good for energy clearing:

Positive Pagan Shower Ritual

Showers can be useful for removing negative energy, and sometimes they're the only option if you don't have a tub. Place the herbs you want to use for your intention in a small mesh bag and hang it off the showerhead so the steam helps activate the herbs. You can also create your own scrubs from natural ingredients.

Items Needed:
⅓ cup sea salt
⅓ cup Epsom salt
6 oz. of oil (almond, coconut, olive)
9 drops of essential oil (lavender, mint, lemon, or grapefruit)

Mix all the ingredients into a beautiful jar and keep it in your shower for when you want to wash away the negative energy from the week.

The shower is also a good place to visualize all the negativity washing down your body, past your feet, into the drain and away from you. As you feel the water cascade down, say out loud, *"I wash away all that does not serve me, all negativity, any darkness directed my way, all those whose energies are attached to me. So mote it be."*

Declutter Keep your bathroom items pared down to essential items if possible. The less clutter there is, the less there is to clean up. Think of your bathroom as a serene place and add items that enhance the serenity. Organize your makeup and grooming items so there's not a frantic search for something when you need to get ready.

Cleanse The bathroom is a great space for plants, so get a few bits of greenery if you can. The plants will naturally purify the air. If you don't have space, use a natural spray and air the room out often to keep the energy fresh. Wash your towels regularly, replace your toothbrush when you recover from illness, and keep whatever you use to wash your body (pouf, washcloth, or loofah) clean and fresh so that whatever touches your body remains as clear as possible.

Draw Out the Vibrancy This room is very functional, so what can you add to make it more vibrant? Plants, candles, and sturdy artwork are all great additions. Smoky quartz is a good crystal to keep in the bathroom, as it promotes positive thoughts and emotional calmness.

Protection A good sprinkling of salt or a sprinkle of Florida Water is useful for this space, as well as a more permanent sign of protection, such as a horseshoe or hamsa. You can find a shower curtain or towels that incorporate protection symbols or keep a bottle of protection oil to use as necessary.

Protection Oil

Items Needed:

1 oz. carrier oil (olive or grapeseed oil are good choices)

4 drops basil essential oil

2 drops pine essential oil

3 drops geranium essential oil

1 drop mint essential oil

Mix all of the ingredients together and place them in a small glass container. Apply to your pulse points as needed, as well as on the back of your neck to keep your back protected.

MAILBOX

The mailbox may not get much attention, but it is a magical place where you can receive items such as packages and letters! Sure, we may also get bills, but let that be a reminder to go paperless as much as possible to help our environment.

Do a quick mailbox ritual after you've cleaned it by offering thanks for the postal process and note the usage of the space as a giving and receiving area. Ask that your mail bring good tidings and offer gratitude for the mail carriers and the work they do, as well as protection for them as they go about their routes.

Declutter It is worth doing a quick dust and cleaning of your mailbox at least a few times a year.

Cleanse Cleanse it with Florida Water, salt water, or use sacred smoke or incense.

Draw Out the Vibrancy Make sure any lettering or numbers are clean and visible.

Protection Get a small, inexpensive piece of green jade to keep in your mailbox, as it is considered a good luck and protection stone.

YOUR WALLET

Your wallet is a sacred tool. You carry paper and coins that are exchanged for items. You may have photos in it that are sacred to you, as well as business cards or information of people that are important to you, your life, and your work. So why is this sacred receptacle usually overflowing? It's worth the effort to keep your wallet cleaned and organized, as well as streamlined. Grab your wallet now and ask yourself a few questions to get this sacred tool back to its magical state.

First, do you even like your wallet? If not, plan on getting a new one. Is your money all jumbled, crumpled, and overflowing? Smooth out the paper money and place it in numerical order. This is a sign of respect for the money you have and can help bring in more abundance to your wallet. Put any overflowing change into a jar you can keep wherever you drop your keys and daily items. That money can go to charity or savings: your choice. That way, the magic continues.

Also keep a bay leaf in the coin compartment of your wallet, or alongside your paper money, as they are known to draw in abundance. Give thanks for all that has already transpired with the wallet and give thanks for all future abundance. There! Now your wallet feels fresh and recharged. Notice what a difference it makes. You can also do the same with pocketbooks, messenger bags, and backpacks. Whatever you carry with you can be part of your magical, Positive Pagan tool kit. Think of it: a master carpenter or chef doesn't leave the tools of their trade all over the place in a haphazard fashion, do they? Do the same with the items you use most, as they are part of your magical life.

Declutter If you collect receipts, gather them and put them in an envelope or file folder. Make it a habit of emptying your wallet of extra pieces of paper weekly.

Cleanse A dab of Florida Water will work, as well as a solid cleaning with a soft cloth.

Draw Out the Vibrancy Get some "attracts money" incense and pass your wallet through the smoke, setting the intention for it to bring abundance into your life.

Protection Florida Water does the trick here as well.

YOUR IMMEDIATE SURROUNDINGS

The definition of surroundings is "the things and conditions around a person or thing." The "things" are the items in your life. The "conditions" are how you go about your day and the environment you find yourself in, whether it be in your bed, your car, your work environment, your socializing, your hobbies, how you spend your time, who you spend your time with, which social groups you surround yourself with, your online community, your alone time, and your spiritual community.

Your surroundings affect how you feel. Simple concept, right? Yet so many people feel "stuck" in their environment, but live in messy spaces, work in draining jobs, have toxic friends, and wonder why their life doesn't feel great. We can't fix it all, but we can start and work on one area before moving onto the next.

Surroundings include how you move in the world. Do you move about in a harried scurry, or do you plod sadly on a regular basis? Take a moment to notice how you are at this very moment. Are you in a happy mode, or clenched tightly? Are you slumped or hunched over, or sitting up excitedly? Do your shoulders droop and does your face feel tight? Take notice of your body and your aches and pains. Are you surrounded at this moment by items you love looking out at nature? Or are you in the busy hum of a coffee shop? Think of which surroundings make you happiest:

it could be nature, a quiet library, your sanctuary of a room, or a cozy kitchen.

Journal Prompt

Time for journaling! Write down five surroundings that make you feel happiest. Describe all aspects of these environments, utilizing all your senses.

Are you having trouble deciding? Spend some time ruminating on this. I emphasize that surroundings are very important as a Positive Pagan. Make it your goal to spend time at least two or three times a day in some of your favorite spaces. For me, it's a walk in a nearby forest, in front of my altar, sitting in my living room, gazing out at a mountain, at my desk writing, and people watching in my favorite coffee shop. Those can change as my circumstances change, but I also take note of how I physically feel during those moments: relaxed, fluid, happy, content, at peace, comfortable in my own skin, languid, and centered.

You can probably look around and see a few choices you can make for the better. Mentally go through a typical day and see what you can switch out for better items or discard.

Grab your journal and make a list of at least six things in your life that you can change in your day-to-day life, whether it be cloth napkins for paper towels or a filtered water pitcher instead of plastic water bottles. Be inspired to do more.

Bonus Journal Exercise

Make three columns. One column will be your present surroundings, the second column will be what you'd like to change, and the third column will be how you'll make the changes. Which change will you put into action first?

Cleansing Your Body and Spirit

Now that we've discussed your surroundings as a Positive Pagan, our focus turns to cleansing your body and spirit. Not just physically cleansing your body as in ritual baths and showers, but focusing on your body as a whole: mentally, emotionally, spiritually, energetically, and socially.

The beauty of Paganism are the actions we can take to move energy and make a difference. We have our rituals and spellwork, and energy sources other than ourselves via the moon and nature that can boost our actions. Then we can use these actions to make a difference in our lives and others.

BE GENTLE WITH YOURSELF

The first action in cleansing your body and spirit is simple: love yourself. Loving yourself may seem so simple, or something you feel you already do, but to examine yourself honestly and truthfully takes a bit of work. If you've never done it before, it may seem daunting, so be gentle with yourself. This examination may reveal some truths that perhaps you hadn't thought about yourself or you worry too much about yourself that you lose sight of actually taking care of yourself.

Self-care is more than eating chocolate and taking baths (although those are important too!). It involves taking time to feel really comfortable with yourself, and to face yourself with all the facets that make you uniquely you. The following ritual is something you can do as a first step in loving yourself. It's a good ritual to do first thing in the morning, but it can be done anytime you need a boost. The key element in this ritual is to set aside time to do it, especially the first time, so you can savor the experience.

Positive Pagan Self-Love Ritual

Items Needed:

A mirror

Body brush or loofah mitt

Sunflower oil

A glass of water

If possible, do this ritual in the bathroom, but if you lack space or privacy in the bathroom, do this in your bedroom or a space you can move about in private. You will want to do this ritual with little to no clothing.

Look in the mirror and really look at yourself. Focus on what you love about yourself, whether it be your eyes, your complexion, your strong legs, or your capable hands. Take note of all of it, and if it is uncomfortable, make note of it and move on to the next step. If you feel uncomfortable with this part of the ritual, try it again a few more times, lengthening the time you spend each time until it's pleasant for you.

Now smile at yourself, stretching the corners of your mouth in a happy smile. Smile at that person in the mirror and take note of the effect on your body.

Pick up the body brush or loofah mitt and gently rub it on your skin in leisurely circles. Start with your hands and then move up your arms to your shoulders. Rub gently across your shoulders and down your belly. Move onward to your thighs and down to your feet and then finish by stroking up and down your legs.

Next, take a bit of the sunflower oil and rub it into your hands, arms, legs, and all over your body. Using circular motions, gently rub the oil in and feel the warmth of the motion, savoring the feeling of touching your skin.

As you do this, say the words, *"Today I remember myself with this act. I stand tall in this space. I accept this act of love for myself. I lean into the universe and all its beings with this action. I receive all acts of love and pleasure with gratitude."*

As always, tweak these words to suit your own way of speaking if you would like. Let these words be a springboard into more self-affirming words and change as needed.

The sunflower oil isn't greasy, and it feels warm all over your body, similar to a hug. Hug yourself if you'd like with gratitude for this ritual to feel your skin and love yourself. Drink a glass of water for hydration.

Positive Pagan Nourishment Ritual

Items Needed:

Comfortable blanket

Favorite beverage

Candle and matches

Journal or notebook and pen

Along with self-affirmation, what you put into your body is important. We all know to eat better, eat healthier, and to drink lots of water. Along with making better choices, take some time to figure out what really nourishes you. When you are nourished, whether by food, beverage, or activities, there is a sense of contentment and deep satisfaction. When you are feeling depleted, it is easy to reach for something quick and possibly not as good for you, food and otherwise. Here is a ritual that you can do that will provide a reference in those moments of depletion and overwhelm. This ritual can be done at anytime, but the best time is when you don't have anything else to do so you have time to ponder.

Get cozy with your blanket and favorite beverage. Cast a sacred circle, calling on your guardians and ancestors to help inspire you as you partake in this ritual. Light the candle and take out your journal to write down, off the top of your head, all the things and moments that you find nourishing. A good book, a film, art, nature, travel, a certain meal, specific beverages, activities, etc. The possibilities are up to you. Are there places that nourish you? Friendships with certain people? Note how your body feels as you list these nourishing ideas and memories. See how many you can list and refer to this list when you feel depleted. Once the list seems complete, open your circle with gratitude and thanks for the possibilities.

CLEANSING YOURSELF MENTALLY

Do you ever feel like there is so much clutter in your brain that you can't take in one more bit of information? Or that you find yourself focused on the same thing over and over? These are signs you need to cleanse yourself mentally. A walk in nature can really clear out the cobwebs and clutter, and you can also pick up trash during your walk to do something good for the environment. Other suggestions are meditation, listening to music, reading, creating art, cooking, making puzzles, volunteering, and sleeping. You can also try a guided shamanic journey as a way to cleanse yourself mentally. It is very much like taking a mental vacation. Guided journeys are found on YouTube or you can check your local community to see if in-person guided journey sessions are available.

Therapy is also a good way to clear yourself mentally. It can be so freeing to have an objective person help you to discern the things that bother you and help you figure out ways to heal.

Cleansing Yourself Emotionally

If you find yourself overwhelmed by emotions, deep breathing and meditation can help provide a bit of stability. Journaling also helps with processing emotions, as well as a good screamfest into a pillow, exercising, and spending time doing things you love. At the next Full Moon, do the following ritual to let go of the things that no longer serve you.

Full Moon Releasing Ritual

Items Needed:

One 8.5 in. x 11 in. piece of paper, torn into squares

Pen

Cauldron, fire pit, or fireplace

Matches

Small treat

Water

At the Full Moon, spend time thinking about what no longer serves you, and write them down on individual pieces of paper. It can be anything from a bad habit to toxic interactions with certain people, to your frustrations, fears, and grudges. Write it all down and read over your list. With each entry, say, *"I release you!"* very emphatically, and put it in the fireplace, fire pit, or cauldron to burn. Light the fireplace with matches.

Offer gratitude for the opportunity to let go of all the items listed.

Once you are done, take a deep, cleansing breath,

Smile.

Eat your small treat to ground yourself after your ritual.

Drink your water. Make sure your fire is completely out before you go elsewhere.

Other ways to cleanse yourself emotionally is to volunteer, garden, hug a tree, or write all your feelings in a letter. Don't hold back, and don't worry about grammar and punctuation. Put the letter away and read it during the next Full Moon. See how you feel, and if you've moved on from what you wrote. Then burn your letter, letting it turn to ashes.

CLEANSING YOURSELF SPIRITUALLY

If you feel disconnected from your spirituality, or if you feel disgruntled with your spiritual community, the best way to cleanse yourself is to go on a spiritual retreat. As in, retreat from it all and take a break from your spirituality! Cleanse yourself with incense and sacred smoke, surrounding your body with the smoke. Move forward from that moment, taking incremental steps back into your spirituality. Wipe the slate clean and start with writing down the basics of what you appreciate about your spirituality. Then integrate them back into your life, one at a time. If you feel certain things need to change, then do so. If you are a person that needs community, look around to see what you can find, whether online or locally. If you prefer rituals, step back and focus on rituals that you can do yourself and see what that brings into your life. Take it all down to the basics; then build it back up.

Other ways to cleanse yourself spiritually is to learn about other spiritualties. Expand your knowledge of the spiritual world, and perhaps find something that resonates with you as you explore.

In addition to ritual baths, use water to cleanse yourself spiritually. Is there a local lake you can plunge yourself into for a quick dip? Water is a threshold for many things, and very apropos when it comes to spirituality. If there is a local spring or waterfall, go to that location and use those moments to set a demarcation line to your spirituality.

Spiritual Water Ritual

Items Needed:
Water (from a local source, moon water, spring
    water)
Small glass bottle with lid
A sprig of rosemary
A thin strip of cotton cloth
Rose quartz (small piece)

This ritual is quick and will create a visual reminder of your spiritual cleanse. Each person has their own spiritual journey with no timeline, but this will serve as a visual reminder of your spirituality as you proceed forward.

Pour the water into the small glass bottle. Add the rosemary sprig. Take the small strip of cotton cloth and speak words of intention into it. Words of what is spiritually important to you. For example: charity, kindness, service to others, ritual, serenity. When you feel complete, tie the strip of cloth around the bottle and place the lid on top. Place the bottle somewhere you can see it often and put the rose quartz in front of it. When you feel back on track with your spirituality, empty it onto the ground, offering thanks for your journey.

Cleanse Yourself Energetically

The most effective way to cleanse yourself energetically is with movement! So jump up and down, shake off the dregs of what you feel, laugh, stretch, run in place, sing loudly, and take a drive with the windows down to blow fresh energy your way. Or try ringing bells or banging pots with sticks.

Tree Energy Ritual

If you can get outside to move, here is a ritual you can do for a quick cleanse:

> Items Needed:
> *Local park or natural area*
> *Trees*
> *Bottle of water*
> *A small container of nutrient-rich soil*

Head out to your local natural area or park with trees, carrying the bottle of water and small container of nutrient-rich soil. As you walk in nature, focus your attention on the energy you feel from the trees. Take some time touching the trees. When you feel moved to do so, hug a few trees. Really hug the tree, wrapping your arms around the trunk. Be very still and note the energy you feel. When you feel your energy has shifted, offer thanks by pouring some water at the roots, and gently pat some nutrient-rich soil there. Verbally offer thanks to the trees and bring the containers home with you to recycle.

CLEANSING YOURSELF SOCIALLY

If your social circle makes you feel not so great about yourself, or you roll your eyes and wonder why you just wasted time with them, then that's a clear sign it's time to cleanse yourself socially. Sometimes people don't because they are afraid of being alone, or they feel obligated. Any of those feelings resonate with you? Then it is time to cleanse yourself socially.

How do you do that? Take some time for yourself and step back from those friendships. Give yourself time to evaluate what brings you joy from that relationship. If you realize that there is nothing, or you feel too uninspired to seek out new friendships, then find yourself your new best friend: YOU. Yes, make yourself your own best friend. How would you treat your best friend? Where would you go and what would you do? Take a few weeks to be really nice to yourself and love your own company. If your friendships don't reflect how well you can treat yourself, then it's time for a change.

Being a Positive Pagan encompasses the people around you who support you in times of trouble, support you when you're blue, understand your quirks and interests, and are genuinely happy to be around you. You deserve nothing less from your friendships.

The caveat here is to be discerning, because sometimes our friends go through bad times themselves, and they can't be there for you. Or a friend is going through difficulties in their lives, and everything's upended for them. That is vastly different from someone in your social circle who takes, takes, takes, and rarely asks how you're doing.

As with the other cleansings, it is best to clean the slate, step back, evaluate, and see which qualities you'd like in your friendships. To do so, make a list of the qualities that are important to, whether it's being supportive, caring, humorous, or respectful.

To assist you with this process of loving yourself as a best friend, use this spell bag to generate even more self-love as you explore this deep friendship:

Self-Love Spell Bag

Items Needed:

Small cotton bag with drawstring (or a cotton handkerchief)

Rose petals

Rosemary

Lavender

Lemon balm (if you can't find lemon balm, substitute a bit of basil)

Small piece of rose quartz

Take a small pinch of each of the herbs and place them in the cotton bag or handkerchief. All these herbs are good for radiating love, so place the rose quartz in the middle of them, set the intention of some good, solid self-love, and close by pulling the drawstrings of the cotton bag or tying a knot in the handkerchief.

FACING THE PAIN

Now onward with cleansing your spirit. There is always a balance to the light, the understanding that there comes a time for darkness. To ignore or deny this is to not have a full appreciation of the light. There are days when life is overwhelming, the world seems chaotic, and we can't seem to move out of bed or off the couch. It is okay to do so, despite the world nagging us to "achieve!" Please be gentle and forgiving of yourself when that happens. Being positive requires a steady flow of energy, so on days when you feel drained or much less than positive, take the time for yourself to recalibrate.

Facing the pain of your life is not done in a few easy steps. It requires more steps than this book can encompass. What eases you on your journey are the moments you hold deep in your heart, the memories that make you smile, and the joy and satisfaction you find in your day-to-day life.

Taking care of yourself needs to be your priority. That is a very, very important concept to absorb and practice! So many times we put ourselves last because we want to be helpful, or we have a lot of responsibilities. It can feel like a lot of work to put yourself first, especially when we are used to putting others' needs first, so start small. Carve out an hour or two for yourself weekly, and gradually build it up for longer periods. Fill that time with what you love to do. Turn off your phone (if possible) and enjoy the gift of time.

When the world feels overwhelming, make some time to meditate. Resolution can be achieved during meditation, and at the very least, you have carved out precious minutes for yourself. This meditation is for those days when you feel lost, a failure, not sure of where to turn next, or overwhelmed by life. Read it first to get the gist of the meditation. Then as you meditate, follow the flow of where it takes you. Don't worry about missing details, or if it's done perfectly. Your intention is what will guide you through this space.

The Overwhelmed Meditation

Items Needed:

Quiet spot

Items you love

Soothing music

Seven-day candles (or candles of your choosing)

Cozy blanket

Water bottle

Journal or pad of paper and a pen

Sit in the quiet spot that you consider safe and soothing. Surround yourself with the items you've chosen. Turn on the soothing background music, light the candles, and cover yourself with your cozy blanket, sitting upright with legs crossed or uncrossed, whichever is more comfortable. Just make sure your back is supported.

Breathe deeply for a count of four.

Breathe deeply for at least three cycles of in and out.

Begin by imagining yourself at your favorite place. The beach, the mountains, a city, wherever you feel happiest. Really feel that you're there, walking quietly in your happy place. Take notice of everything around you, no matter how little it seems. Do you see a leaf or a stone there? Don't pick them up, just make note of it. As you move through the space, look ahead and see a cozy, warm light glowing. Similar to candlelight, that soft, warm glow draws you closer. Feel the glow of the light until it completely surrounds you. Feel yourself in that light as if it is your sanctuary and bask in its glow.

Take a moment to check in with your feelings, emotions, and perceptions. Just take note of them, as if you were watching words travel across a screen. Take another deep breath. Recognize and embrace each one as it passes in front of you. That anxiety you felt this morning? Give it a gentle hug. Let it keep going. That sadness you felt at an email you received? Another gentle hug. That moment with your friend where it felt like she didn't get you at all? A heartfelt hug. Move on through all those pieces of today and give them hugs in the glow of the light.

When you feel like you are at the end of all those feelings and emotions, take another deep breath. Give thanks for everything you feel, and let it wash over you like a waterfall. Feel the cascading down your body, all the way past your feet and into the ground. Let that water seep into the earth along with all those feelings. Send it deep, deep into the ground, past the flooring, past the foundation, deep into the earth. Think of it as compost for the earth, and let it spread out far and wide. Feel the release within your body and give yourself a gentle hug. Smile, letting the corners of your mouth lift upward. Now take your shoulders and lift them all the way up to your ears. Hold that tension for a count of ten, and then release it with a huge sigh. Blow all the tension out, as much as you can.

When you are ready, head back from the light into your happy place. Rejoice in all that you see around you. Feel yourself return to your present space. Don't open your eyes just yet. Instead cup your palms over your eyes as you open them, letting the light in slowly. Take your time to rejoin the present. When you are ready, take your hands off your eyes and take another deep breath. Drink your water until your thirst is quenched.

Grab your journal and write down all that you saw. Don't worry about the coherence, as it can be a list, a sequence of words, a Venn diagram, whatever you feel called to write and/or draw. When you're done, put it to one side. Take some time to think about all the different items, and in your relaxed state, notice if any meanings come to you. If not, don't worry; you can come back to it after a day or two and see what comes up.

If you want to do some divination with oracle or tarot cards in this relaxed state, then do so. Don't be worried about layouts. Let your intuition guide you. Look at the cards displayed and take a picture or draw the layout in your journal. Try to discern what it means, using the guidebook that accompanies your deck to help. This too can be looked at after a few days to let the message digest.

Vent to Your Deity/Deities

Your deities are your allies, helping you along in life or bringing things to your attention. They get it; they see you struggling. So why not pour your heart out to them? Rage, rant, cry, scream, yell, talk as long as you want. Always be sure to leave an offering on the altar first, of course (out of gratitude and manners), and just go to town. Sure, it seems a bit odd to talk out loud to seemingly no one, but they really are listening. If you feel too shy to vent out loud, then write them a letter or compose one in your journal. Messy handwriting or composing it on your laptop doesn't matter. The point is to get it out of your inner self into another container. Don't let anything fester in your system; process it and move it out. Emotions trapped in the body can lead to illness and a poor mental state.

If writing isn't your thing, then create a drawing or a collage. Find different ways to express yourself, such as fiber arts, dancing, creating art with nature items, or making up a song. Record it somewhere and play it back when you feel strong enough to do so. In working with your deities, you can also sit still and listen. Listen to what they tell you. It may be one word or phrase, one small feeling, or one small voice telling you something.

Listen, and let your relationship be reciprocal.

For those who prefer a ritual, here is an option.

Vent to Your Deity Ritual

Items Needed:

Deity statue or photo

Seven-day candle (your choice of color or one that corresponds to your deity)

Food and beverage offering

Flowers or item from nature

You may already have an altar set up to your deity, but if you don't, set these items on a cloth on the floor or on a low table.

Light the candle and arrange the food and beverage offering.

Instead of casting a circle, cast a bubble for you and the deity. Call them in, offering thanks, and imagine the white bubble surrounding you and this sacred area.

Take three deep breaths and place your hand on your heart.

Ask your deity for help and guidance for what is bothering you.

Look at the statue or photo of the deity and gaze upon it with friendly and loving eyes. Reach deep down within yourself and be truthful. Say all that you need to get out of your system, not worrying if you sound strange or what anyone else would think. Focus all your energies on speaking freely. Take as long as you wish.

If you feel that you would like some action from your deity, then ask politely. "I would like … (the following to happen)." It is not a wish list, but an action or two that you'd like to see happen in your life.

When you are done, again offer thanks and gratitude. Place your hand over your heart and say, *"It is done."* That marks a line between this moment and moving forward.

Snuff out the candle when ready and do this ritual daily. I often do my rituals for either three or seven days because for me three is a magical number and seven is for commitment. Use your intuition on how many days you want to continue; you will know when you're completely done, and this one ritual may feel complete for you. Light the candle daily in offering to your deity and continue to leave a beverage or small treat for your deity in gratitude.

If you journal, please do so. Note how you felt during the ritual, the thoughts you had, the ideas that popped up, if you felt your deity's presence, and what you asked for help with, if anything.

Spellwork

Spellwork is effective because of this: action helps you feel better. One action moves you toward more, and spellwork is an entry to more positive things happening for you. How affirming it is that you can move energy to get things done! It also takes you outside of yourself, because for spellwork to be effective, you have to focus and turn your attention outward, find the items you need, do a bit of research if needed, and follow your intuition as you work toward your intention. The beauty of ritual items, the glow of the candle, calling in the ancestors and guardians as you cast the circle, and then releasing them after the working. Letting go of all that you can't control, and letting the deities and universe do its part in your spellwork; it is a feeling like no other.

Ritual

Ritual turns the mundane into magical, and sometimes it only takes a bit of thought and intention. Look at your routine during the day and see if there are activities that you do on a regular basis. From the number of times you stir your coffee, to your morning and evening routines, time spent at your altar, and all the rhythms of your day.

Humor

Humor can brighten your spirit quickly. There is something magical about laughing so hard that your belly has a slight ache, or your face hurts from smiling. Laughter is magic and movement.

With so many movies at our fingertips, go seek out comedies. Modern, classic, silent, cartoons, comedy specials, and more. Look up jokes online. Watch YouTube if you don't have streaming services. Get together with friends and laugh. Dark humor counts, so get those face muscles working with smiles and laughter. Go see local storytelling and comedians. Comedy can give you perspective and laughing gets you out of the darkness. Find your favorite childhood cartoons and let them brighten your life again. Find your favorite comedian and look for their recorded performances. If you don't have any favorites, then start with some classics like the Marx Brothers or ask for a friend's favorites to get started. Google "top comedians" and work your way through that list.

Wait

Things may seem bad now, so wait. Just wait. Waiting seems passive, but it is an active choice. Choose to wait, to look ahead, to wait for things to get better. You know that adage, "Will it matter a year from now?" Use that as a guide to get you through some dark times.

Waiting is being present, and being present is hard work. Looking ahead can be a survival mechanism. Looking backward can be a good marker of how things have and can change. Realize that nothing can change what has happened, but you can affect your future, so focus on the power and intention of that.

It can be hard work being a Positive Pagan, especially with the world the way it continues to be. It can be daunting and seem useless, but there is a certain power and strength to being positive. We all feel darkness, and life can get to us and knock us down. Resilience is part of the Positive Pagan's tool kit, so know that your journey into darkness is acceptable. Just be sure to find your way back when you can.

THE TRAIL OF BREADCRUMBS

Although being in the present is very grounding and healthy, sometimes your past pops up in your life. Instead of scurrying away from it, take some time to partake in the Trail of Breadcrumbs. It's a ritual that asks you to look backward at your life to see the connections you've made and the paths you've taken that lead you to this moment. It involves some clear-eyed self-realization, so do this when you are feeling centered and grounded. The fun thing about this ritual is you can do it with a close friend who really knows you, or you can do it yourself.

Trail of Breadcrumbs Ritual

Items Needed:
Turmeric, sage, and rosemary
A small bowl
A cup of peppermint tea
Candle, candleholder, and lighter
Paper and pen

Take a pinch of each of the herbs and place them in a bowl. Make yourself some peppermint tea. Light the candle, take some deep breaths, and begin by taking a whiff of the herbs. Take a sip of the tea, letting the mug warm your hands, and check to make sure you are grounded and centered. If you are not, then do so now. Gaze into the candle to put yourself in a meditative state.

This next part you can do with a friend, or you can do it by yourself. Reminisce. Look back at your life as dispassionately as possible, from the earliest memory until now. Go with what your brain picks out as the highlights and write them down. Write them in chronological order or write them down and then put them in a timeline.

When you feel complete, take a look at the memories. Do you notice a pattern or any similarities? Is there a trail of breadcrumbs that lead you to, "Aha! This is why I do what I do!"

Write the trail of breadcrumbs down and stop when you feel comfortable.

This is a good ritual to do every once in a while, and it's helpful to do with a good friend who can remind you of certain patterns and behaviors that you have. This ritual brings awareness, makes note of your patterns, and is a way to accept responsibility for your actions. Along with being gentle with yourself, being aware helps make change possible.

DO THE WORK

These three words are powerful. Do the work. Do your magic, your ritual, your spellwork. Despite how easy it can be to do nothing, you will also receive nothing from that. Rest when you are weary, but know that you are a powerful being that can make things happen.

So get active and do something. Not sure what to work on, or how to? First, figure out your biggest issue or problem. Then listen to your intuition and gather your supplies. Not hearing anything? Feeling stuck? Do research or read a book. There is so much information out there, and you will know what resonates for you.

Work with the lunar cycles to work toward a better outcome. Doing the work is also learning more, gathering knowledge, putting your magical knowledge into use, and moving energy toward your desired results.

You can begin by organizing your supplies. Throw out anything old, no longer useful, or empty. Recycle, if possible.

Spend time at your altar and devote some time with your deities. Leave them offerings and talk to them. And do good work in your community.

Work on yourself and make plans, lists, and resolutions.

Let "do the work" be your daily goal, mantra, and belief.

Journal Prompt

Time to get your journal out! List five different activities you do on a regular basis. Then add a little ritual to them. How can you make the mundane more magical?

Now, look that list over and start with your morning. Do you have a routine? Or do you bolt out of bed and rush to work? Try setting the alarm a bit earlier so you can establish a different routine than the one you are presently doing. Prepare a delicious breakfast, a healthy smoothie, or a special kind of coffee, practice meditation, spend time at your altar, read a chapter of a book, journal, or exercise. Maybe you can try greeting the sun and see how that feels. There is something special about the sun rising up and peeking out at the start of a morning. Wear a special robe or cozy pajamas as you do so. Voilà! A ritual. Add a special drink or a breakfast snack and make it even more magical. If you are slow to wake in the morning, then take your time getting out of bed. With your eyes closed, visualize how you want your day to go. Don't make it stressful with a list of to-do's; instead concentrate on how you'll feel and what you'd like to wear to make it a magical day. Perhaps that piece of jewelry from your family that you forget to wear. Wear it today.

During the day, you can add rituals to when you get in your car or travel to work, when you have a meal, take a bath, and an evening routine. Any of these can have a ritual added to them. The most challenging part may be slowing down to acknowledge the action. We tend to race through our day, or we lurch from one task to the next. Moving in a mindful way all of the time can be challenging, but worth the effort. When you do, life flows in a way similar to water. Time seems to slow down and expand, and things get done more peacefully. Enjoy that time and remember it when things get dark periodically.

Living Community

How do we create and exist in community? If you have created your own positive bubble and space, how do we let other not-so-positive family and friends enter and visit? Do we let them in, or stay in our Positive Pagan bubble, reaching out as needed, limiting our social interactions? Do we just grin and bear it? Do we shun them? This can be a dilemma.

Family, friends, co-workers, and other members of the community can be a challenge when it comes to being a Positive Pagan. Sometimes these interactions with others can feel beyond challenging; there are even times it can feel paralyzing. How do you deal with endlessly negative people in your life when you're doing your best to get through each day? In addition to feeling challenged and unheard, you may also feel frustrated, angry, and defensive.

The first thing to do when you feel this way is to breathe. Take a deep breath right now, as you read this; breathing helps. Then work to release the tension present in your body. A few more deep breaths, and then consider perspective. Being in the moment and present is optimum in most situations. But there are times when other people intrude on our space and leave us feeling unsettled and struggling to maintain a positive perspective. At these times, it's best to mentally step back, observe, and listen.

Stepping back mentally takes you out of the feelings this person engenders and gives you distance. Observe how that person inhabits their body. Are they tense, upset, seemingly ready to burst? It probably has nothing to do with you. Think of their life and their circumstances, past or present. Maybe they've been going through a hard time, have had past trauma resurface, or are in a momentary bad mood. After you take that deep breath, observe, take some time to pivot, and listen.

LISTENING

Listening seems so simple, yet most of the time we listen to reply. Or we are eager to help, waiting for the person to stop talking so we can leap in with our suggestions that will make everything better.

Try not to do that. Actively listen to the person.

And then respond.

Respond by first letting them finish talking. Then repeat what you heard back to them. That act alone can make the person talking feel seen and heard. They might relax and pause, appreciating someone actually heard what they said. You can ask curious questions about what they've said, actively taking an interest. Then tell them how it affected you or that their story reminded you of something similar that happened to you. And if they ask for your advice and suggestions, offer it then, and only then. People just want to be heard, and true listening takes practice.

ACCEPTANCE

The quickest way to diffuse all that negativity is to realize that you can't change that person, and the choice to change is their own. That in itself is a challenge because acceptance can be a difficult journey. Let go of the idea that the person will change their ways, that you will be heard, and that your relationship will be different.

Acceptance is like letting go while riding a roller coaster, feeling scared but trusting the process. Once you are ready, an acceptance ritual can help you move into greater ease within yourself. This ritual can be used anytime, so keep it in mind for those moments when you do not feel that acceptance within yourself.

Acceptance Ritual

Items Needed:

White candle and candleholder

Lighter or matches

Rose quartz

3 Tbsp of each: Chamomile (for calm), Tulsi (for balance), Hawthorn (for comfort)

Small Mason jar

Strips of paper and a pen

Cauldron

Set your items in front of your altar, in a quiet space, or outside.

Light the candle.

Get yourself comfortable, taking some deep breaths.

Close your eyes and visualize the negative person you are struggling with at this time.

Place your left hand on your heart and grasp the rose quartz in your right hand.

Take three more cycles of deep breaths.

Put the rose quartz down and place all the herbs in the Mason jar.

Cover the jar and shake, mixing the herbs together.

Open the jar and take deep breaths of the scent.

Take the slips of paper and write down all the attributes of this person that you are frustrated with in either words or sentences.

If at any point you feel grief, give yourself a gentle hug.

Take the lighter or matches and light the papers on fire, dropping them into the cauldron.

When you finish burning the papers, open the Mason jar and take out a pinch of herbs.

Place the herbs in your palm and take another deep breath.

Gently blow the herbs away. If you are inside, blow them into the cauldron.

Sit still for a while. If you feel grief, comfort yourself with gentle hugs, or place your hand on your heart.

When you feel ready, clean up your area.

Keep the herbs in the jar to use as a tea or to add to your bath when you feel sad about this person. Add the cooled ashes from the cauldron to your garbage or bury them away from your home.

BOUNDARIES

Boundaries are a useful part of the Positive Pagan tool kit. They can be challenging to put into place, especially when you're not used to doing so, but they are ultimately worth the effort. Next to shielding and grounding, boundaries are essential, but sometimes people don't know how to set or enforce them. Protecting your energy as if it is your most valuable treasure is worth the time it takes to learn how to set boundaries.

It begins simply.

First, start with saying this word: *No.*

Say it a few times.

Then try, *"No, thank you!"*

It gets easier, I promise.

Boundaries can seem hurtful or strange to other people, especially those who are not used to them. If you have a hard time saying no to things, examine why. Do you feel you're missing out? Do you relish being needed? Do you think people won't like you if you say no? Do you feel like it's your job to take care of everyone? If you answer "yes" to any of those questions, then you may indeed have challenges with setting boundaries.

It's time for some self-work. Begin by forgiving yourself if you feel like this is a failing. It's not a failing at all and is pretty common in this go-getting world of ours. If you want to change, then do it one step at a time.

Try pausing before you give an answer to a time commitment. Say, "I will get back to you later" if you're not comfortable with giving an immediate answer. Listen to your intuition and note how your body feels when you consider this option. If something doesn't feel right to you, say no. It may take a few times to get there, so give yourself some space and try again when you can.

Boundaries are a good thing. Think of them as an invisible gate or shield around you. They keep all the negativity out, and you can go about your business. Another way to set the boundary is to remove yourself from the person. Stay out of their vicinity as much as you can. If this is someone you care for deeply, then another boundary is to tell them how their negativity affects you. This may feel scary, but you can do it via a written letter, email, or text. It may not change that person's mind, but you won't know until you try. You saying something sets a boundary.

Once you've stated how you feel (it is truly about you, not them), then remove yourself as much as you feel necessary. If this is a co-worker and you can't remove yourself from their presence, then actively start looking for a different department or job.

You can also try spellwork to remove that person from your sphere. I like to use the word "sphere" because it encompasses all that is in your life, envisioning everything in a bubble. So something or someone may not be in your vision or life on a regular basis but has enough presence in your sphere to affect you.

Banishing spells or a spell to move your co-worker to a different job could be effective. The best part is, once you've set the Black Salt Banishing Spell into motion, you can forget about it and let the energy take care of the situation. The key is to focus on what YOU want: to remove this person from your sphere. This does not involve something negative or harmful happening to them. It's like letting the inevitable happen, and this spell is a little boost. Setting this intention is the key component to this spell working. Be very clear about its purpose as you set this intention. Not "I want xyz to happen," but "I would like xyz removed from my sphere." Then step back and see what happens.

Black Salt Banishing Spell
Items Needed:
Small piece of paper
Pen
A bag of black salt, approximately ¼ cup

Write this person's name down in quantities of three, as three is a magic number. I prefer nine, so I use that most often. Write their name three times in one direction. Move the paper in a counterclockwise direction one turn and write their name three times across it again. Then do that one more time. Fold up the paper and put it in the bag of salt and pop it in the freezer. Be sure to label it with at least the date so you can keep track of who's who, in case you do more than one!

If this doesn't work, then it's time to escalate. I caution you to only use this if you need some added oomph to get this person out of your sphere. The intention is the same as before, with no harm or harmful action involved. It is very effective, so please use sparingly. Directing the energy toward that person with this spell is ongoing, so when done, be sure to dispose of the ingredients properly. They're best buried away from your home.

Banishing Spell

 Items Needed:
 Pen and paper
 1 glass jar
 Vinegar
 Crushed red pepper
 Hot sauce
 Thumbtacks
 Nails
 Shards of glass
 Any other sharp object, such as a nail or thorn
 Black candle (optional)

Do this on the Dark Moon (the night before the New Moon). Write the person's name down in quantities of three (as listed above in the Black Salt Banishing Spell). Say whatever words you like while doing this as a sort of mantra: *"I want this person gone from my life, I want this person gone from my life, I want this person gone from my life"* is an example. Fold up the paper as tightly as possible, place it in the jar, and cover it with the items listed. Whatever calls to you intuitively, add to the jar. Remember, this spellwork is not to harm the person, but to remove them from your sphere. Place the lid on the jar and shake it. You can burn a black candle on top of the lid to seal the work. That part is optional. Again, see what you're called to do. When done, place the jar in a dark space, such as underneath your sink in the farthest corner. Leave it there and forget about it. Your work is done, so mote it be.

FRIENDS

What if you have an endlessly negative friend? The one who always complains, focuses on how horrible their life is, and never has anything remotely positive to say. I've seen people struggle with these friendships, feeling a sense of obligation and unable to distance themselves. Feel sympathetic, but it's also time for some self-protection.

Ask yourself, "What do I get out of this friendship?" That may take a while to process because you may have a long, shared history. If you ultimately want to keep the friendship, set time boundaries, and remove yourself if you feel physically or emotionally overwhelmed in their presence. You can keep a boundary setting spell bag on your person when you encounter your friend to keep the positive energy flowing out and their negative energy from permeating you.

Boundary Setting Spell Bag
Items Needed:
Small cotton bag with a drawstring or a cotton handkerchief

Any one of the following boundary-setting crystals:
lapis lazuli, malachite, pyrite, black kyanite, or
black tourmaline
A pinch or two of each of these herbs: rosemary,
nettles, and yarrow

Place the crystals and herbs in the cotton bag or cotton handkerchief. Pull the drawstring closed or tie the handkerchief in a knot. Keep it in your pocket or close to your heart. Wear it all the time or have it readily available for the times you spend with this person.

If you spend time with friends and family and want to spread subtle positivity, then make some Positive Pagan tea, and share it with everyone, including yourself! It is delicious iced or hot.

Positive Pagan Tea

Items Needed:
Tea kettle or small pot
Water (filtered or spring, if possible)
2 small handfuls and a pinch of lemon balm
1 handful of nettle leaf
1 cinnamon stick
A pinch of rose petals

Bring the tea kettle or small pot of water to a boil. Throw in the herbs, turn off the stove, cover, and remove from the heat. Steep for about 15 minutes. Strain and pour into mugs, adding honey, preferred sweetener, and lemon as needed.

Stovetop Potpourri

Another way to invite positivity into your home gathering is to have stovetop potpourri simmering. The smells invite good conversation and an atmosphere conducive to positivity. Be sure to keep a pot designated for stovetop potpourri, as you will want to keep a pot simmering year-round. It's also good for keeping moisture in the air.

Here are two to use: one for the warmer months of spring and summer, and the other for when it is cold and chilly during autumn and winter. You can use the same pot and ingredients for a few days before discarding the ingredients (hopefully into a compost pile). These recipes are both good to use for three to five days.

Spring/Summer
Items Needed:
2 lemons, sliced
3–6 sprigs fresh rosemary
3–6 small pieces fresh ginger, sliced

Put all the ingredients into a pot and cover with water. Simmer, adding more water as needed. Don't forget to turn off the stove when you're done!

Autumn/Winter
Items Needed:
Orange peels (1–2 oranges)
6–9 cloves, whole
1 tsp cinnamon, powdered or sticks
1 tsp nutmeg, freshly ground

Put all the ingredients into a pot and cover with water. Stir once and simmer. Add more water as needed. Don't forget to turn off the stove when you're done!

Positive Pagan Elixir

Another way to keep yourself inwardly grounded and able to deal with less-than-positive people is this warming honey mixture that you can add to your daily water. You can add it to a warm glass of water as a sipping tonic throughout the day or add it to hot water and lemon to help with a cough and scratchy throat. A table-spoon in either drink is recommended.

Items Needed:
2 bowls, 1 small that can fit inside a larger one
Hot water
3–4 Tbsp raw honey
1 fresh knob ginger, peeled and finely chopped
¼–½ tsp cinnamon, ground
1–2 Tbsp lemon juice, freshly squeezed
¼–½ tsp black pepper, freshly ground
Small jar with lid

Spoon the honey into the small bowl and place it into the larger bowl. Pour hot water carefully into the larger bowl until it's about halfway up the side of the smaller bowl. Let the honey soften for about 5–10 minutes. Take the smaller bowl out and add the remaining ingredients. Set aside for about 30 minutes. Then spoon the ingredients into the jar and cover it with the lid. Keep at room temperature for up to 4–6 weeks.

FAMILY AND ANCESTORS

Family can be harder to navigate because there are so many emotions and loyalties involved. You might still be in the closet as a Pagan, depending on your spiritual upbringing. The best thing to do is model positive behavior. Again, the focus is on you. Who wouldn't love being around a Positive Pagan such as yourself? You are healthy, vibrant, loving, in charge of your life by the choices you make, grounded, protected, working your spells, cherishing nature, and more. What's not to love? So take care of you first and limit exposure to your family as much as you can and realize that you don't have to like your family members.

It's easy to love your family because they're your family, but it is perfectly acceptable to not like them as people. It takes a burden off of you to realize this. You have to work with people you don't like sometimes, right? Same with family members. If you don't like someone, don't take what they say to heart. It is a boundary and a way to protect yourself from their energy. Sometimes acknowledging that you don't like a particular person is freeing, and also sets a boundary. Your body may acknowledge this boundary before your brain does. Our bodies know if we don't actively like someone; so pay attention and observe what happens. Does your body get tense? Does your jaw ache from tensing it, or from biting your tongue around this person? Reducing your presence around that person can help. If that's not possible due to family obligations or other reasons, then limit your exposure as much as you can and be comfortable with placing your needs first.

Journal Prompt

Time for some journaling.

Which boundaries do you have trouble setting? What actions, after reading this chapter, can you take to set boundaries? Which parts of being in a community do you enjoy? Which parts do you dislike?

CHAPTER

7

Resistance and Freedom

Ah, the joys of resistance, especially when you resist something you know will benefit your life. Why do we do that? Probably because it takes work and self-examination, and it's easier to not do something in the hopes that it goes away.

Resistance is a huge mountain to overcome, and it can be difficult to take that first step. Once we finally manage to get to point A, the journey seems a bit easier to get to point B. It seems as if many of us feel this way on a regular basis.

You recognize the feeling of resistance: that clench in your stomach, the hackles rising on the back of your neck, the feeling of stopping while in forward motion. The times where anything else takes precedence over what you need to do. Distraction abounds. Resistance within yourself is a journey many of us encounter and can take varied forms: physical, emotional, mental, and spiritual.

FACING RESISTANCE

Reacting to resistance depends on the circumstances. You can pivot and move around whatever you resist. Maybe it will get done later. Things get put off, and ultimately you hope it will go away. Or you decide to face it head on, looking deep within to figure out why you are resisting. That can stop you in your tracks because it requires the untangling of so many feelings, emotions, and experiences.

Dealing with resistance is not an easy or simple thing to do, but the rewards are worth it. Journeying through resistance can bring you to the other side with a feeling of accomplishment. That sense of euphoria, freedom, and pride that you worked through the mountains of resistance and are now clear and moving forward. It's like climbing up a steep mountain, feeling the strain and work of your body, and reaching the top to take in the wondrous view.

How do you begin this journey of moving through resistance? Begin simply.

As with other processes as a Positive Pagan, begin with gratitude. It puts you in a better frame of mind, and from there positive resolutions can flow. If you are full of negative thoughts and energy, then the resistance digs deep with no forward motion, and nothing will likely get resolved. A quick gratitude list, or review of your Gratitude Journal, can put you in a more open frame of mind. It's one step forward. Here is a quick ritual to do before tackling something you have been putting off. It puts you in a more open and receptive frame of mind, and from there, hopefully action will flow.

Gratitude Before Resistance Ritual

Items Needed:

Yourself

Outdoors (or open window if you can't make it outside)

Take a few deep breaths to center yourself, and gaze at your outdoor environment. If you can make it outside, great! An open window works just as well. If your view isn't stellar, look up at the sky. The point is to be inspired by your view.

Take a few more deep breaths and start listing all the good things that are going on in your life. Begin with your senses if you have difficulty starting a list. Add your best friend, your pet, the latest book you read, or a delicious meal you ate recently. List items until you feel complete. Notice how you feel. Are you smiling? Is your body feeling less tense? Do you feel energy flowing? Give yourself a positive affirmation, whether it be a mental or physical hug, a few words of encouragement, or an exhale of relief. Now you are ready to move onward!

Journal Prompt

What five things are you resisting? Are you resisting physically, emotionally, mentally, or spiritually? Write down what first comes to your mind. Then take some time to put them in the order of importance to you.

The Resistance Walking Meditation

Once you have clarity, it's time for action! Taking that first step can be daunting, but there are ways to ease into what's needed to remove the resistance. A walking meditation can help determine what is your prompt for this resistance.

It's best to do this meditation outside, but if you want to walk around your home, it will work as well. Be sure to hydrate before you begin and add some soothing background music if you want.

Stretch your body, reaching up as far as you can.
Swoop down and touch your toes. Feel the energy

flow through you from the top of your head, down through your body, continuing down to your toes.

Begin walking by taking comfortable strides and taking deep breaths. Deep breathing in and out. When you have achieved your steady pace, direct your mind toward your favorite open space in the world. As you walk, think about what you are resisting in a detached manner. Don't attach any energy to it.

Think about possible solutions to what you resist and try to figure out what you need to make it happen. More time? Effort? A better frame of mind? Notice your thoughts as you ponder on your resistance.

Up ahead, in the middle of the open space is a wooden box.

Walk toward the box, but not in a hurried rush.

Open the box.

Inside the box is a piece of paper with something written on it.

Take a deep breath and look at the paper.

What does it say?

Is it a picture or words?

Or does the writing disappear?

Close the box and walk back toward where you came.

When you find yourself back where you started, close your eyes.

Offer words of gratitude, hand over your heart, and then open your eyes.

Back in the present reality, observe what thoughts pop into your head.

Journal about this meditation and do it as often as you need to when resistance pops up. Don't get discouraged if you don't see any words at first. Something may bubble up in your thoughts later, so stay open to the experience. It's often a word of whatever blocks you from moving forward.

BLOCKS AND OBSTACLES

Resistance is blockage. So when faced with a blockage, what do you do? You can go around it. Maybe. But sometimes there is no other way but through. You may know what's blocking you, and the magic of what you're trying to get to is on the other side, whether it be a new life or a new project. Working through resistance is most effective when you use magical tools. Place some road-opening magic within as you create some Obstacle Removal Salt.

Positive Pagan Obstacle Removal Salt

Items Needed:

2 oz. coarse sea salt

1 Tbsp each:

Coffee grounds (for boost)

Marjoram (for happiness)

Crushed red pepper (to blast through blockages)

Dried lemongrass (to banish the blockage)

Bowl

Glass jar with lid

Mix all the items together in a bowl, stirring counterclockwise to enhance blockage removal. Speak words of obstacle-removing intention over the bowl. Stir in multiples of 3 (3, 6, 9) until you feel it's complete. Place everything in the jar and seal it with its lid.

Use this salt for times when you need an obstacle-removing boost. You can sprinkle it around an object that is causing you resistance (such as exercise equipment, an item from a stalled project, etc.) or hold the jar when you need a visual and physical boost to move ahead.

Memory Rosemary Tonic

Part of being a Positive Pagan is the aim of being truly comfortable with yourself. This is a lifelong journey that you're on, so be kind to yourself if you're frustrated where you are in your life. It may be that some of your resistance is grief or trauma that has resurfaced, so try to learn to surf the waves instead of allowing them to overtake you. Take a moment now to visualize yourself riding the waves. It's a better feeling, isn't it? It requires a safe space and a deep core knowledge that nothing is permanent. Patience and trust are key, with yourself most of all.

When memories seemingly come out of nowhere to distract or stop progress, this rosemary tonic is useful to help wash away the lingering residue of those recollections. Rosemary is the herb of remembrance so the action of washing away, plus its magical use, is a powerful ally in clearing this type of blockage.

Items Needed:
9 sprigs fresh rosemary, finely chopped
About 3 cups filtered or spring water
Saucepan with lid
1 Mason jar with lid
Apple cider vinegar

Strip the sprigs of rosemary and chop them as fine as possible. Add them to the water in the saucepan and cover with the lid. Boil for around 10 minutes. Allow the mixture to steep for 30 minutes before straining. Pour the rosemary water into the Mason jar and fill to the top with apple cider vinegar. Keep in your shower or near the tub to use as a rinse after you wash your hair. As you rinse, visualize all the negative energy and memories washing away from you down the drain. This mixture should be good for around 3 months.

You Should

One of the most frequent words that pop up when facing resistance is "should." Nothing can paralyze actions more than that one simple word. It can stop a person in their tracks, make them feel they are doing something wrong, and can feel incredibly restrictive. If you feel the same, here are a few steps to help:

1. Don't do it. Whatever it is that you are resisting, stop and don't do it for a while. Take a breather.

2. Acknowledge that you don't want to do it, and that there are reasons why you don't. Acknowledge this in your journal, meditations, or thought processes. Sometimes this action frees you from the avoidance.

3. If what you resist is something you don't want to do, but has a deadline, such as taxes or a project, then break it down into small, manageable steps. Try not to get overwhelmed at the big picture of the project. Focus on the steps as you do them, one by one. If the steps seem overwhelming, then focus on what you can do in one twenty-four-hour period, and no further. That is much more manageable than the entirety of what overwhelms you.

Recognize your limitations, and don't feel bad about them. Only you know what you can handle. Your mental health is your priority, not other people's timelines.

ASKING FOR GUIDANCE

Resistance can show up in different ways in your body. Your body can pick up on what may not be right for you way before your mind does, so you may have physical reactions to resistance that make no sense at the time. You may feel like everything is perfectly fine, and that you have everything under control, including your stress levels. The first thing you can do, which sounds so incredibly easy, is to be still and listen. It sounds like a no-brainer, doesn't it? Yet so many of us don't do it, as we get distracted by whatever catches our attention. We find something else we'd rather be doing, and we don't want to face whatever has been ignored within us. You may feel exasperated or frustrated, which leads to more avoidance. Being still and listening is challenging at first but getting through to the other side is worth it. You can magically support yourself in this process by asking for help from your ancestors and deities.

Ancestor Guidance Ritual

Items Needed:

Altar space, shelf, or tabletop

Candle (either white or black works well, but whatever you have on hand will be fine)

Photo(s) of ancestor(s)

Offering of food and drink (coffee, alcohol, treats, water, bread, or whatever you feel guided to offer)

If you have an Ancestor Altar set up year-round, even better! Place your candle and offering on the altar. If not, find a space to place your candle, photos, and offerings.

(Let me pause here for a note on ancestors. If you did not personally know your ancestors or if you don't have pictures, that's not a problem. You can find an object that represents your family. For example, if your great-uncle was a sailor or baker, and you would like to call on him, then use objects to represent his profession. If you are adopted and unsure, then place a rose quartz heart to represent your ancestors because you were created from generations of love.)

Next, light the candle and gaze into the flame. Ground, center, and be still. With an open heart, reach out to your ancestors and offer them gratitude for your being.

Now, ask for help with what you resist. Talk as if you are talking to a friend. Let them know what you need help with and all the things you are struggling with before asking for guidance and help. When you feel you've expressed everything, sit back and listen. You can do this with your eyes closed or open but feel open to the experience and see what bubbles up. It may be a phrase, a memory, or an option that you hadn't thought of before. If you hear nothing, don't despair. Communicating with ancestors takes practice, so end this ritual with gratitude and try again at another time.

If you find yourself facing restlessness, mental upheaval, and emotional turmoil, go deeper and practice quietness to get back to center. This is a constant practice, and the results will come more easily the more you practice.

Notice how you might reach for distraction when you're afraid of feeling emotion and divert your attention back to yourself. Does quiet make you feel nervous? Does stillness seem foreign to you? Try it for a few moments at a time and increase the time each session you practice. Be still and listen. Let it be a mantra during these times.

Your intuition could be telling you not to do something for very good reasons, as in it's not safe or helpful for you. It's up to your personal journey to know the difference, and it takes a lot of self-work to distinguish between your intuition, your deities communicating with you, or you talking yourself out of something.

Sifting through emotional sediment can feel like such a slog, but it will be worth it. If you don't feel up to the challenge, by all means see a professional therapist to help you with this journey. There are also spiritual counselors and coaches available, so take your time and choose one you feel comfortable with and whose methods resonate with you. Taking care of your emotional foundation is an important part of remaining positive during offbeat times, so it's helpful to regularly check in with yourself to see if any cracks have formed in that foundation.

RESISTING YOUR DEITIES

Resistance to your deities can be quite an interesting journey, one that can change your life in meaningful ways. People sometimes feel a certain deity calls to them, and they're not sure why. Do you answer? Sometimes people don't. It could be due to fear, lack of understanding of what they are called to do, uncertainty about the unknown, and honestly, doubts about their sanity. When a deity calls, consider answering. It will be quite the journey, and could result with you learning more about yourself, your deity, and your spirituality.

How do you recognize if a deity is calling you? It can be that persistent voice that is not your own, urging you to act. Or a visible sign that shows up repeatedly. There may be resistance to this, and it may be challenging to have the time or bandwidth to deal with deity interactions or requests. Mostly because it's unknown.

You may think: What do they want from me? Why me? What will happen if I do xyz? How can I be sure it's a deity? The list goes on.

The deities may have been trying to reach you for a while. Looking back you might see a trail of messages that you didn't connect the dots with until now. Even if the deities are asking you for a huge, seemingly insurmountable task, pause and listen. Is it doable? What is the reason you resist? You can ask. Answers might include for you to be bolder, to follow your path more definitively, and to do things such as self-improvement, a project, or a career change. It may seem insurmountable, but step back from that fear and look at the realm of possibility. It may take a leap of faith, a series of steps leading to a result, or changing direction from where you thought you were going.

Listening to your deities involves trust. That can be a scary thing if you're not sure what is happening, so take your time until you feel comfortable. When you are ready, listen carefully and take a leap of faith.

A leap of faith may seem like a bottomless pit of "what if?" but if you consider the process like stepping stones, it's a less-scary prospect. Take one step at a time and see where it leads! Don't look at the big picture and know that things can change for the better.

How do you begin working with a deity? As you start any new relationship, put in a bit of effort. Set up an altar, prepare an offering, and set aside some time to truly communicate with your deity.

Welcoming Deity Ritual

Items Needed:

A small table/altar space

Cloth covering or placemat (to protect surface from candle wax)

Item representing the deity (a drawing, statue, or items related to the deity)

Seven-day candle in a color associated with the
deity, chime candle, or plain white candle
Candle snuffer (optional)
Small vase of flowers or greenery
Offering of food and drink (try to research what is
associated with the deity, or regular bread and
water is fine)
Incense or scented spray (this can be considered part
of the offering, or as a way for you to reach a
relaxed state)
Small cushion or something comfortable to sit on

Set up the table or altar space with the items and light
the candle. If you feel called to add other items, then
do so. Breathe deeply and get into a relaxed state and
begin speaking to your deity. Always offer gratitude
for contacting you first, and then just talk. Follow
your intuition or inner voice as to what to say. You can
compose a poem, sing a song, or talk as you would
with a close friend. What is most important about this
ritual is that your heart is open to the experience. You
can say whatever is in your heart if something troubles you. You can even ask for a sign that you've been
heard and acknowledged. Be as authentic, heartfelt,
and vulnerable as you can. If you would like guidance
or direction, say so. Don't be discouraged if you don't
feel you get a response right away. Relax into the open
lines of communication and be alert to the world
around you. Repeat this ritual as often as you feel comfortable. You can check in with your deity as often as
you like, and however you like. Enjoy the journey.

RESISTANCE TO MOVING AHEAD

If you're still not sure of how to move forward, take a look at your past. Think about times you took a leap of faith and recall what happened next. The following is a useful exercise called "What's the Worst That Can Happen?"

Take out your journal and list a few things you've been asked to take a chance on within the past few years, along with the results of taking that chance.

Now, keep the situation in mind as if it was happening tomorrow. Spin it out to the very worst-possible scenario. Be as dramatic as you'd like, and truly go for the gusto. The purpose of this exercise is that it allows you to face your worst fear.

You will either realize that this fear is huge, which you can work on separately, or you will laugh at the extravagance of it and realize that the dramatic scenarios in your head are not feasible. Could the worst-case scenario happen in reality? Look backward to all that you thought would happen in past situations, and realize how things went in a different direction, along with the end results. Could it be that what happened could have proceeded to even better directions?

SHIFTING ENERGY

Laughter relieves tension and it opens the pathway of discovery. Don't rush into the next thing and leave this exercise behind just yet. Look at your fears again and scale back what you think realistically could happen. Write down possible solutions next to your fears. If you are stumped about solutions, then go back to the fear that feels huge. Is it something you can break down into smaller pieces?

Another way to shift the energy of resistance is to take away the option of that very thing you resist. If you take away the choice of not doing whatever it is you resist, then your mind will shift into ways to accomplish the thing you are avoiding. We all have things in our life that we absolutely have to do, so put your object of resistance in that category, and find ways to accomplish what may seem impossible. Be kind to yourself if there are lots of stops and starts as you move along. You always have the option to hit the reset button and begin again. Try it and see!

Inspiration

Inspiration is another way to shift energy around the resistance you experience. You can tap into the positive energy of the internet and social media for inspiration. If you find yourself repeatedly turning to certain people, it's worth performing the magical ritual of the Magic Box of Nine. It can be a powerful visual inspiration that can move you into action. Similar to a vision board, the Magic Box of Nine is a quick shorthand of people you'd like to surround yourself with, including their kind of energy and inspirational accomplishments.

Magic Box of Nine

Take some time to think of the people who influence you most.

Make a list. Include those presently in your life, those you admire, and those you follow on social media. It can also include characters from your favorite books. Narrow down your list to nine people. You can print out photos from the internet or draw or paint the individuals.

Create a photo collage of all nine people and post it where you can see it on a daily basis. Preferably keep it in a place where you create, but it can also be in a spot where you can view it every day. These nine figures of inspiration can help empower you to make change, as they undoubtedly went through changes themselves to reach their pinnacle. (If you're not sure of their journey, this is a great opportunity to learn more about them.)

Keep the collage updated, as sometimes our interests and those who inspire us can change as our pathways change.

Cleansing

Cleansing is always beneficial in shifting energy. If you notice energy feeling static, wonky, or uncomfortable, it's time to cleanse. When the energy shifts, resistance can move into more possibilities.

A few ways to cleanse the energy in your space:

- Sweeping
- With smoke: incense, scented candles, herbal bundles
- A small bowl of Epsom salts: add some rubbing alcohol and carefully light the alcohol with a candle
- Florida Water
- Stomping
- Ringing a bell
- Mopping, dusting, wiping down with a cleansing blend/wash
- Clapping your hands
- Clearing out clutter
- Opening all the windows

In addition to cleansing, strengthen your protection as well. There are many protection sprays available online. Here's one you can create at home:

Positive Pagan Protective Cleanser

Items Needed:

Lemon peels

2 cups white vinegar

Small Mason jar

1 Tsp cleaned and crushed eggshells in a mesh tea ball
1 Tbsp natural salt
Warm water
Small bucket
Large empty spray bottle

Mix the lemon peels and one cup of the vinegar in the Mason jar and store for 2 weeks in a dark place. Strain the mixture and add to the remaining ingredients in a small bucket and mix. Place your hands over the mixture, setting your intention for cleansing and protection. Let it sit for 3 hours. Remove eggshells and pour the contents into the empty spray bottle. Use to wipe doors, doorways, doorknobs, windowsills, and any other area you'd like. Let air dry.

When you change up the energy in your space, take note of how you feel. Are you more energized? Do things now seem more possible? Take advantage of this and move through that energy to what needs to get done.

RESISTANCE FROM OTHER PEOPLE

When you do change your life in positive ways and feel better about yourself, sometimes the people in your life are not immediately comfortable with your improvement. Mostly because you are no longer in the "box" they've created for you. For example, "Oh, xyz is miserable in their job." Therefore, xyz's misery becomes a constant. So what happens when xyz leaves that job and becomes much happier as a result? To others, xyz is seemingly a different person and they're not sure how to react. You changing your life may make them uncomfortable because they don't feel able to change their life, and it was comforting for you to complain together. Friendships can adapt, but sometimes it's not a friendship you created, but rather a shared experience, likely a negative one. Once you don't participate in sharing that experience anymore, the friendship may change or end.

My advice is this: do your best to ground, shield, and center (sound familiar by now?). Focus on yourself and your own happiness. Don't worry about the opinion of others, and do things because you want to, not because you want to please others. The rest will fall into place. Your circle may become smaller, but it will be more authentic and intimate. It's an amazing feeling to have a tribe of authentic, lovely friends.

If you don't have a choice when surrounded by people who aren't supportive or authentic, I suggest wearing a spell bag on your body. It can be filled with lavender (for anxiety reduction) and a good chunk of tourmaline for protection. It may seem a bit harsh to suggest protection, but it's more for protection against their energy than the person themself.

Other things you can do? Wear your protective jewelry and send out love when you're around them. Imagine your love as a beam that comes from above you, filters through you, and comes out through your heart toward the person in question. If you continue to find their presence challenging, reduce your time around them if possible.

In addition to being centered and grounded, focus on your personal goals. If that takes daily meditation, gazing at your vision board every day, or chatting with supportive friends, then do so. Journal your thoughts as well, because that will help process all the feelings you encounter during this transition with your friends.

RESISTANCE TO THE WORLD AROUND YOU

There comes a time when you may feel like the world around you does not fit. You know when a piece of clothing doesn't feel comfortable? Scratchy, ill-fitting, just doesn't feel good. If you're not sure why you have this feeling, take time to take stock of your life. The answers may not come right away. You may not be fully aware of it happening, but somehow something feels … off. It could be that your job, your relationship, your friendships, or your day-to-day life feels meh. It could be the season your life is in, and you need to work on yourself. It could be that your job doesn't suit you, and you feel stagnant, stuck, and helpless. If this happens, be sure to clear the energy around you using your preferred method of cleansing.

Spiritual hygiene is important to keep energies clear and flowing in your environment. Clear your altar and make sure it is free of dust and has fresh offerings. Use sacred smoke to clear your rooms and open the windows to get fresh air flowing throughout. When you are done cleaning, finish up with a ritual bath or shower.

When that is all done, take stock. Go through all the important parts of your life and make lists. Divide each list up into what isn't working, and opposite that, what you can do to make it work. Don't worry if you can't make any of the listed changes just yet. For now, just create a visual. Then put it aside.

Next, energize yourself. A ritual bath should help, but add whatever works for you, including body work, exercise, herbal supplements, and healthy foods. Once you feel more energized, tackle your list. Ready to change jobs? Begin the process of looking, but don't tackle it all at once. First update your résumé, and then start applying. Are friendships bringing you down? Take a break from your friends and focus on yourself. Life feeling meh? Make plans to attend a few events in your area. If you're not up to socializing, then focus on your hobbies and what brings you joy. Learn more about what interests you, whether it be a new hobby or something you've always wanted to learn. Sign up to learn a new language or take an online course. The focus is to act because movement helps you feel better.

From there, make the changes you deem necessary. Use the moon's energy to help you along the path. Remember that the New Moon is good for setting intentions, and the Full Moon is for releasing what no longer serves you.

Writing lists also helps. Jot things down as you remember them, and revel in the feeling when you accomplish them! If the idea of lists overwhelms you, make a visual list of drawings or pictures from the internet to keep you on track. Like a vision board, but more focused on what you want to get done (getting new glasses, scheduling a wellness check, looking at new cars, booking a vacation, finding a new job, etc.).

Follow your passion! If you've always wanted to live somewhere else, start researching. Maybe it's completely unattainable at the moment, but that doesn't mean things can't change. Keeping it in the hum of your life can help make it real. If your passion is opening your own business, start taking courses, find local start-up help, and talk to other entrepreneurs. If cooking and baking make you glow, practice those. Squeeze as much joy as you can out of your days, because honestly, my friend, life is short. We all know this, so start today and you'll have already made progress when you look back at this day tomorrow!

FLIPPING RESISTANCE ON ITS HEAD

Another way to work with resistance is to bring what you want toward you, as opposed to resisting it. This way you focus and direct the energy of what you are trying to achieve toward you as opposed to expending energy outwardly toward what you resist. Resistance can feel like hitting a wall and bringing something toward you feels like opening a door.

Most people consider this manifesting. While manifesting is sometimes misunderstood and thought of as New Age, a simpler way of explaining it is that you use energy to bring what you want toward you, similar in many ways to spellwork. If you keep pushing against something that feels like a wall, your resistance will end up being tired and stagnant. Manifesting isn't just a Christmas list of things you want. It includes goals, plans, and sometimes changing your way of life. Bringing that which you desire toward you requires work and consistency, but it is less exhausting in the long run and your energy will flow more easily. It is so much more than creating vision boards and visualizing. The most effective ways to manifest involve using all your senses. Here are some basic guidelines.

Positive Pagan Manifesting

What you see Visualize what you want to bring toward you by creating a vision board, placing affirmations where you can see them, creating a saying that begins with the words, "I am…," writing your manifesting list for Full Moon rituals, placing your list on your altar, and making room in your life for that which you would like to add. For example, if you want a relationship, make room in your home for one. Make room in your closet, make your bedroom a space for more than one person, and visualize the partner you would like to have.

What you touch Get an object that symbolizes what you are trying to manifest. For example, a rose quartz heart for love, a pen for writing, an art supply if you want to create more visual art, or a gold coin if you'd like to bring in abundance or money for a specific purpose. It helps to have specifics if you're trying to bring in more money, as you could manifest that and be inundated with extra work. You'd have the money, but no free time, so specificity is important.

What you hear Listening to people who inspire you, whether it be their music, audiobook, or podcast, is important in manifesting. Let's face it, if you listen to negative talk or complaining all day, you'll be in a quagmire of negativity, and nothing will flow.

What you taste Can what you taste affect manifesting? It is a bit more subtle than the other senses in manifesting but can be effective just the same. A small spoonful of honey can draw in sweetness and love, while cinnamon is associated with abundance. Do your research and find herbs that correspond to what you are trying to manifest and see what happens.

What you smell Very similar to taste, what you smell can help deepen your manifesting. If roses remind you of love, then add that scent via oil diffusers or place a small dish of rose petals on your altar. Like a muscle that strengthens with repeated use, your senses will reaffirm what you are trying to manifest and will engage you into its creation.

In addition to senses, feel what you're trying to manifest. Visualizing and involving your senses will aid you along the path of manifesting, but if you don't lean into feeling as if what you want is attainable, then none of this will help. Patience is important because what you want may take years. Consistency helps. You may feel as if you're spinning your wheels, but hang in there! Once you have what you seek, you will marvel at the path it took to get there. Enjoy the journey.

Journal Prompt

List ten things you can turn to when feeling positive just isn't part of your day. Use this list as a reminder when you need it.

When It Gets Dark

I t is impossible to be completely positive all the time. Let's get that clearly stated here and now. The balance to light is dark, and as a Positive Pagan you should know that finding that light in the darkness can be a monumental challenge at times. As humans, we may encounter many dark days. No matter how wonderful our lives may look on paper and social media, we don't necessarily share what we've gone through in our lifetime, nor do we know what other people have gone through. We doubt ourselves and feel sadness, overwhelm, and lethargy. Life seems to be going swimmingly and then, out of nowhere, old memories surface. Or we have ancestral trauma wash over us, perplexing and confusing us in its wake. Many of us have dark days that can last for a season or longer, and it can seem like a tunnel we can't escape, no matter what we attempt to do.

There are periods in our lives when gratitude lists are not enough, and times we'd prefer to hide from the world. Our personal lives can affect us negatively, as well as our family, community, and reactions to world events. Healing from trauma can take a long time and can stop you from moving forward in any capacity.

Being a Positive Pagan isn't centered on being endlessly positive no matter what happens. It's more focused on appreciating the light when we find it and finding our way back to a beneficial frame of mind. The way back is not a one-time journey, but a trip we may end up taking often.

HOW TO GET THROUGH THOSE DARK TIMES?

To begin, know that nothing replaces therapy and consulting with your medical doctor if your dark days leave you incapacitated and unable to function. Dark days mentioned here are those periods of spiritual depression, feeling blue, without energy, and stuck. The doldrums. Feeling a bit overwhelmed by life, but still able to function. The dark days when life seems an endless circle of the triple threat of fear, doubt, and anxiety.

There is an ember of positivity inherent in all of us, and to recognize and find that ember is a way back to our center. Life is our journey of always putting one foot in front of the other. It can be as simple as that. One step at a time. Progress is progress, no matter how small that step is in your journey, so give yourself credit for where you are in this moment.

For Positive Pagans, there is an inner spark that somehow keeps us going. It is a small flame that burns within us, no matter how many layers we dig through. We can forget it's there, but when needed, it helps weather the storms of life. Maybe it's determination or a positive attitude. It could be an inner conviction that all will be well, and that things will work for you. If you're having trouble finding that ember, try the following ritual to locate that little burning flame inside you.

Finding the Burning Ember Ritual

Items Needed:

Cozy clothing

A quiet place

Candle, candelholder, and matches

Hawthorn essence (check your local metaphysical shop or find online)

Your journal

Dress in your coziest clothing and find a quiet space.

Place your candle in the candleholder and light the flame.

Take 3 deep cleansing breaths and look into the flame.

Spend some time envisioning an ember deep inside you.

Visualize what it looks like: is it a candle flame, a burning coal, a banked hearth with a few sparks? Do you see the glow and light from the flame?

If you are struggling to find the ember, think of the thing about yourself that you are most grateful for, a small pat on the back that is sorely needed at this time. Something you are really proud of yourself for, whether it be achieving a specific thing or surviving a difficult challenge, or even an activity as simple as making the bed and drinking water today.

Feel the ember glow a bit stronger, and feel the warmth spread through your body. Track the warmth as it courses through your body.

When you feel complete, take 3 more deep breaths.

Place 3 drops of the Hawthorn essence on your tongue or mix it in a glass of water.

Hawthorn is an essence that is helpful for opening up and emotionally healing the heart. It's useful for those who have difficulty shifting from busy activity to rest and stillness. You can add taking three drops to your daily routine or keep it for this ritual to use when needed.

Offer thanks and cherish that ember within yourself.

Repeat this as often as needed.

Each time after the ritual, take out your journal. List five things you are proud of yourself for, with no thought of what someone else would think about your list. This journal entry is all about what you think. It doesn't matter if what you choose are big things or little things. Draw your favorite symbol around your list, and smile. You have accomplished something! Add to this list as often as you'd like.

"I AM"

Another way to find that spark of positivity is to use these two powerful words in your daily self-talk: *I am*. If that seems too simple at first glance, consider the words that follow "I am." How do those two words make you feel? How would you finish that phrase? Repeating the phrase "I am ..." followed by what you consider your strengths, is a daily habit that can enhance your personal well-being. By regularly saying these words, you build a shield of positive self-affirmation that helps during the dark days.

A few suggestions:

I am strong.
I am compassionate.
I am healing.
I am resilient.
I am powerful.

I am talented.

I am loved.

I am present.

In addition to writing, stating these words is a quick ritual to get you back on course if you feel off-kilter and aimless. It can be done quickly, or more elaborately as you have time. With practice and repetition, you can snap your fingers, say the words, and get yourself back into a positive space.

The Powerful I Am ... Ritual

Items Needed:

Candle and candleholder

Matches

Rose quartz crystal

Paper and pen (a journal is also fine for this ritual,
*   as are markers or other creative implements)*

Get your supplies and find a peaceful spot to do this ritual. Light the candle in the candleholder.

Take 3 deep breaths to center yourself while holding the rose quartz crystal.

Visualize the words I am ... and see what comes up in your thoughts. Think of all the things that you are, the essence of you, and your favorite attributes of yourself. Envision a warm, glowing light around yourself. Write down the phrase: I am .... Come up with at least two or three ways to complete that sentence and say them to yourself as a mantra over the next few weeks. Stand a little taller, straighten your shoulders with your chest out, and take deep breaths as you say to yourself, I am ... Give yourself a mental or physical hug if you feel called to do so, and repeat this ritual as often as necessary.

An addendum to this ritual is to write the different I am ... statements on pieces of paper that you can affix to your bathroom mirror or somewhere you go daily, perhaps the cabinet door by your coffee maker.

DEEP DIVE

Taking care of and loving yourself is a directive we often hear about, but maybe don't follow. The next step on this journey is to examine your personal world. What is your daily routine like? What gives you energy? What depletes your energy? What do you do to truly love yourself? And while we're on the subject, how exactly do you love yourself? For many people, loving oneself comes down to basic maintenance, perfunctory habits to get your basic needs taken care of, and that's about it. Do we take time to really like and enjoy ourselves? We spend the most time with ourselves, so this relationship with yourself should take priority.

Have you ever met someone that didn't know the first thing about themselves? No matter where you are in life, getting to know yourself is a worthy journey to undertake. Why do you like the things you do? What brings you joy? What do you definitely dislike? If you can't answer those questions, it's time to get to know yourself! Once you answer those, more questions and answers will follow, answers only you can give. So enjoy the process and dive deep.

Many times we get distracted and look anywhere and everywhere else to avoid focusing on ourselves. Keeping the focus outward doesn't leave a lot of time for focusing inward, does it? In order to deal with the dark times in our lives, we need to be fully comfortable and accepting of ourselves, so we can navigate through these times. It's not something that's achieved overnight, so it takes a bit of patience and faith. Journeys always begin with a first step, so take your first step by taking a loving look at yourself.

Time to journal with a focus on creating an inventory of what you like about your favorite person: you! In your journal, write down at least five things you love about yourself. Note how you feel when you look at this list. Is it difficult to identify what you like about yourself? Start small and think about the things you feel you do well, how you contribute to your community, and how you move through the world. Is that a little easier? If this list still stumps you, put it to one side and move onward with some acceptance rituals.

ACCEPTANCE

A big step in self-love and care is *acceptance*. It seems so simple, doesn't it? Acceptance of yourself seems like a no-brainer. Even if you consider yourself low-maintenance, or a person with simple, basic needs, you may not be accepting of yourself. You may think you should do or be more. You may give yourself a hard time for whatever your perceived weaknesses are, whichever projects you didn't get done, or however your physical body presents itself at a certain moment in time. More of whatever you are not at the present. Sometimes we ignore ourselves, focusing outwardly on our family, other relationships, work, and the world.

If you haven't given the concept of self-acceptance much thought, try this quick exercise. Hold your gaze in the mirror for as long as it's comfortable. Was it brief? If this is a challenge for you, take action and move some energy through the following acceptance rituals. Incorporate the practice of holding your gaze in the mirror until you reach the point of content, smiling satisfaction with yourself in the reflection. Feel that quick rush of love that perhaps you reserved for others in your life, and revel at the warmth of that love directed at yourself.

Acceptance can take some time, so don't think this is a race or has any timeline. Give yourself credit for what you have achieved, and don't be harsh with yourself for what you have not. Accepting yourself is an important part of the foundation of being a Positive Pagan because if you are fully yourself, positivity flows more easily. Resistance is the opposite of acceptance. Think about a frozen lake or stream. That is what resistance can feel like. Everything feels clenched up, negative thoughts run through your head on a constant carousel, and exhaustion creeps in. When the water melts, the water flows more easily. Move some energy and try to embrace yourself.

Acclimate yourself to saying positive things about yourself. Send those words and energy outward from your mouth to the sacred space that is your bath or a place where you feel safe. Sometimes the basic need for us as humans and Positive Pagans is to feel safe. A simple four-letter word that conveys much. We can go through so much of our lives not even realizing that we feel unsafe, so try to find that place via the following ritual.

Safe Space Ritual

Items Needed:

You

Whatever cozy is for you (cup of tea, blanket, soft clothing, etc.)

Your favorite crystals or stones (enough to make a circle around you)

Journal and pen

This is a simple ritual that is best performed when you are feeling at ease and is not to be done in a hurry.

The items listed above are guidelines, so surround yourself with whatever YOU deem as safe and comforting. It could be done at your kitchen table or in your bed. It could be outside. Form a large circle around you with your favorite crystals or stones. Substitute flower petals, sticks, stuffed animals, spoons—whatever moves you at that moment.

Close your eyes and take some deep breaths. Count to four as you breathe in and out through your nose. Spend time thinking about the last time you felt truly safe and comfortable. Take your time in this process, as you may not easily remember. Was it childhood? Time spent with your best friend? In the embrace of a loved one? Out in nature?

Once you find the spot in your memories where you felt safe, shrug your shoulders up to your ears, clench your shoulder muscles tightly, and release. Take one more deep breath.

Go back to that space in your memories and engage your senses. Be present in that safe space for a few moments. When you feel ready to be back in the present moment, journal all the things you noticed about being and feeling safe in that moment.

Savor that memory and soak up all your senses in that moment. What were you doing, feeling, tasting, smelling, and hearing?

Then ask yourself:

What in your present day reminds you of that safe place?

Can you recreate that moment? Can you find something similar?

Write down everything about that moment in your journal. Make sure to note as many details as possible.

Are there any items you can add to your environment that you don't presently have?

Make a list of items you need to add to your environment.

When you feel complete, close your journal.

ESTABLISH A ROUTINE

Routine helps with feeling positive because you are doing (hopefully multiple) things to help you feel better. The key is to find a routine that fits YOU, so it doesn't feel like a chore or burden. Finding this routine is a journey of knowing yourself, which yes, takes a lifetime. So know that one of the first steps into the backbone of this routine is acceptance. Be prepared for things on your list to change as you evolve and be flexible. As humans, we can be so hard on ourselves if we feel like we're failing. Take time to give yourself credit for what you have done instead of focusing on what you haven't accomplished.

Being a Positive Pagan is a regular journey of going back to your center over and over again. You may get discouraged and think, "Again?!" It may feel like a constant course correction. Using these tools, rituals, and actions regularly will help you get back to center more effectively and quickly.

As a quick refresher, try to incorporate your days with:

- Meditation
- Deep breathing
- Grounding, shielding, and centering
- Protection
- Hydration
- Spiritual practice
- Gratitude

Once you have a daily foundation, use it as the backbone of your day and a comforting place to return when you feel overwhelmed with life. Things you can do without much thought but are good for you at the same time. Action helps you feel better, so it's the first step in getting through the dark times.

PROCESSING TRAUMA AND TRAUMATIC EVENTS

There can be times when you're doing all the work and everything seems to be going swimmingly, and out of nowhere, past traumatic events bubble up. It can feel scary, confusing, and frustrating.

If you know the source of the trauma and feel as if it's something you can deal with yourself (as always, therapy is recommended when the load is too much for you to bear), the following ritual can help ease some of the bewilderment and panic when this situation arises.

Calm in the Storm Ritual

Items Needed:

You

Water

Candle, candleholder, and matches (or battery-operated tealight)

Tissues (in case of weeping)

Paper and pen

A quiet space

Doing this ritual requires a space in which you feel safe to express yourself. If that is your bathroom, bedroom, or out in the middle of a field, find that spot and bring the items with you. Take some deep breaths to begin. Drink the water to get hydrated and light your candle or switch on the tealight.

Now, close your eyes and meditate.

It may be hard to quiet your mind, so picture yourself on an elevator.

Take a deep breath and sink into the present moment.

The elevator is descending. You feel the motion and see the numbers going down.

Keep taking deep breaths.

Once you feel you're at the bottom, start at the top of your head and unclench your body, part by body part.

Let your body feel like it's floating.

Let your emotions wash over you.

If you feel like crying, do so.

If you feel numb, acknowledge it.

If you feel anger, recognize it.

Remember: Vulnerability is strength.

Be open to what courses through you.

When you feel complete, open your eyes and take time to reintegrate into your space. Journal. Reiterate to yourself that it is okay to feel your feelings, and truly honor that acceptance.

ANCESTRAL TRAUMA

There are times when trauma bubbles up that is not yours. You recognize that it's not your own, mainly because you inherently feel it's not yours, yet there is an echo of remembrance in it. When turmoil hits, you may wonder where the emotions come from, especially if you thought you had dealt with them long ago.

When this happens, it's time to sit still and listen. Truly listen and see if you can pinpoint the origin of these feelings. If you have an ancestor altar, spend some time by it. If not, spend some time with your ancestors by looking at photographs and going back through your memories.

Ancestral trauma can be carried forward in our DNA, so if you know your family history, and this makes sense to you, connect with your ancestors by doing the work.

The work includes spending time with your ancestors and talking to them as if they are right in front of you. Set up a simple ancestor altar with some photographs and a candle. Sit with what you are feeling and see if it has a glimmer of their origin. In order to free yourself from the familial burden, a cord cutting ceremony can help. Cutting the cord to that trauma via a physical act can help process the emotions and shift your energy to a more positive space.

Ancestor Cord Cutting Ritual

Items Needed:

Ancestor candle (if you don't have one available,
use a plain white candle)
A long string or piece of yarn
Scissors

If you have an ancestor altar, great. If not, place a photo or an array of photos from your ancestors on a table or bookshelf. An alternative is to write your family name(s) on a piece of paper to represent from whence you came.

Light the candle, take some deep breaths, and gaze into the candle for a few moments.

Wind the string around the photos or piece of paper with one end in your left hand, the hand of receiving.

Thank your ancestors for all they have given you, such as physical attributes, fondness for certain foods, or any part of your nature and personality that you instinctively know comes from them.

When you feel ready, cut the string.

Offer affirmations of release, gratitude for being in a safe place, and gratitude for physically severing the ties to your ancestral baggage. Be proud of yourself for breaking a cycle, even with this one specific action.

NATURE IS THE LIGHT IN THE DARKNESS

The most consistent and helpful way to push back darkness in your life is to be out in nature. Going for a walk or hike, hugging a tree, or planting a garden are all ways that help move you physically and mentally past some dark times.

Consider the elements as you seek a path through your darkness.

Earth Ground yourself by walking barefoot on the grass, spend some time with your back against a tree, hug a tree, touch dirt, plant a garden, or learn to identify plants on your next walk.

Air Blow bubbles, go for a drive and feel the wind through open windows, fly a kite, gather feathers (wash your hands afterward), stand outside when it's windy, or climb a mountain and feel the wind at the summit. Spray some natural scents in the air to create a sacred space around you.

Fire Light a candle, sit around a bonfire, burn incense, or get an oil lamp and watch the flame. Enjoy the warmth of the sun on your skin (wear sunscreen) and spend some time in an open field on a sunny day or enjoy a picnic.

Water Take a bath, fill a pot with water and play in it with your hands, or go to a beach, lake, or stream. Fill your water bottle with gratitude and mindfulness (for all those who aren't able to do so). Sit by a waterfall and immerse yourself in the experience, noting all your senses involved.

JUMP INTO A NEW SPACE

Sometimes when it gets dark, a simple activity to move yourself and your energy is to jump. Jumping may seem silly, yet consider this: people jump over a broom after a handfasting or wedding, jumping into a new reality as a couple. You can do the same using your broom, a stick, or a line in the sand. Think of it: moving from one space (the present) to another (the future). Physical actions move through your body and up to your brain, so before you dismiss it, give it a try and see how you feel afterward.

HELPING OTHERS

When you feel like you can't find a way out of the darkness, think of ways to help others. It doesn't have to be a grand gesture or a huge commitment of time. You can leave flowers or a baked good for your neighbor, teach a skill to a young relative, or volunteer at a local organization. Getting outside of yourself will engage your monkey brain with something besides the endless circle of thoughts you may find yourself trapped in.

Those thoughts can keep you trapped in that spiral, and although you may not want to do anything, put one foot in front of the other and move toward helping someone besides yourself. Do one thing for someone else and then you can get back to whatever you were doing before. See how you feel at the end of one act of kindness, and then decide if you want to do another. Chances are, you might like that feeling.

We especially need you in the Pagan community. Be part of a ritual, helping make the world a little more magical and a little less mundane. You can teach others what you know, learn something new, make friendships, and expand your horizon.

FIND AND KNOW YOUR SUPPORT

The phrase "your vibe attracts your tribe" is often true, but when the darkness hits, interacting with people can be the last thing on your mind.

You may notice there are not any group rituals in this book. Being a Positive Pagan is an individual journey, so all the work and rituals are designed for you to get yourself into a positive space, not the crowd. Why is that?

Think of your Positive Pagan self as a light, and that light shines outwardly. Your vibe of being positive, open, and at peace with yourself will attract other people who share similar outlooks. Can you be grouchy and have unhappy days? Sure. It's the human experience. But turning the mundane into magical, feeling happy with your life choices, and moving forward in life, helping others, and improving yourself will result in a support system of others who share this outlook.

Just like water, friends and tribes will flow in and out of your life. The key is to keep an eye on yourself, and yes, be selfish. Selfish with your time, energy, emotions, and life. Put yourself first and focus on getting yourself in the best space possible. The rest will flow like water. Consider this if that doesn't seem possible: Is what you're doing now working for you? If not, and you find yourself frustrated, get back to the basics.

Surround yourself with what makes you happy.

If you don't know what makes you happy, start the journey of figuring it out.

Love yourself. Truly love yourself, all the bits and bobs, flaws, and not so wonderful aspects.

Change what you can and can the rest.

Don't worry about what other people think of you. That worry can take up so much valuable time and energy.

Have zero expectations and realize life can only go up from there. This is not defeatist; it's a way of looking at things, events, and happenings with a sense of wonder and surprise. If something turns out better than you expected, great! If not, what have you lost? A bit of disappointment, and then you move onward.

If you find you're surrounded by stagnant people, lessen your contact with them. Stagnant meaning all they do is complain and make no choices, no movement, and no decisions. They stay essentially trapped in a world of their own making, and they don't move on from it. Just as you flow from the positive changes in your life, so should your friends and tribe, too.

Journal Prompt

Get out your journal. List some of your favorite people in the world. It can be those you know personally, some that you follow on social media, and those in the world trying to make a difference who you admire. As you list them and you find yourself smiling, list what about them inspires you and makes you happy.

Refer to this list often. If it changes, note what you're drawn to: is it their generosity, humor, or their exciting life events? Ponder on what you can add to your own life from their traits. Also list shared values that you find important. Refer to this list when you feel alone or unhappy and view this list with gratitude.

CHAPTER

9

Living Full Circle

What does living Full Circle entail? The journey of being a Positive Pagan is an ongoing one. Similar to the Wheel of the Year. Each year, as the Wheel of the Year turns, we find ourselves with a Sabbat that focuses on specific intentions and focus. The key is to celebrate the focus and familiarity and finding renewal each time.

TURNING THE WHEEL

Let us begin with birthdays and setting intentions for the coming year. As you turn another year older, ask yourself: What do I want my life to look like a year from now? All changes require a bit of planning and time. Finding the new in each year can be a fun and exhilarating challenge. Maybe you want the coming year to be a Year of Health or a Year of Travel. If the thought of a whole year ahead is a bit overwhelming, take a piece of paper and write down words that appeal to you. Think of what you want more of in your life. Is it health? Deeper relationships? Finding your life partner? Different work?

Then, break it down into manageable goals. If health is your focus, what could you accomplish in a month? Three months? Six months? Breaking it down into smaller time increments can feel much more doable, and easier to plan. Follow that up with a way to track your progress. Do you prefer lists, journals, or using social media to be accountable? Is tracking your progress on social media inspiring or terrifying? Are sticky notes helpful?

Another way to find the new in the coming year is to create vision boards.

Vision Boards

Items Needed:

Magazines

Photos and printed quotes from the internet

Poster board or 11 in. x 14 in. canvas

Glue

Stickers, stick-on jewels, washi tape

Markers, gel pens, crayons

Beginning a vision board takes a bit of writing and some decision-making. Spend some quiet time thinking about what you want to accomplish in the coming year. Start with three to nine ideas, and then find magazine photos or images online you can print, cut, and arrange on the poster board or canvas. Enjoy making the collage! Make it something that is really pleasing to you and place it in a location where you will see it daily. Use it to inspire you and make a point to spend time gazing at it daily.

If a collage isn't appealing to you, this method can be applied to a journal or notebook. Write about your goals and check in with what you've written regularly. Your journey to a year of health can be taking a walk to participating in a marathon by your next birthday. Start with a 5K and keep moving forward.

The key to planning is to *be kind to yourself*. Some journeys have interruptions and detours. If this happens, put it aside for a while and come back to your goals when you can.

Sometimes we can be very hard on ourselves if we find ourselves slipping into behaviors that we have worked hard to distance ourselves from. I've found a method that really resonates and helps with times I backslide.

1.0 VS. 2.0 VERSIONS OF YOURSELF

When you look back at your choices and behaviors, you can clearly see how far you've come! Especially if you're working on yourself, including Shadow Work. Shadow Work is everything we can't see in ourselves. You must look at yourself deep within, including the behaviors you exhibit that you don't particularly like, such as jealousy or envy. It takes time, and some hard work, so if you've been on this journey with yourself, kudos. We all are human, so if we find that kind of behavior rearing its head in our more up-to-date and enlightened selves, call it "(insert your name) 1.0." For example, when I find some old messages or behaviors showing up during emotional or tense times, I call that Lisa 1.0. It helps me to distinguish that way of being from my present state, with a nod at the work I've done. Present-day me, after therapy, Shadow Work, self-help, and self-care, is Lisa 2.0. The newer and improved me definitely got an upgrade in programming.

Try it and delineate that version of yourself. We embrace all of ourselves but be sure to acknowledge your progress. You can certainly add different versions beyond 2.0 that acknowledge your growth, but I've found it incredibly helpful to have a short-hand term such as version 1.0 to categorize your prior behavior when it pops up. My 1.0 behavior encompasses control, jealousy, negative self-image, and the spiral of behavior that led me to seek therapy and help. When your issues threaten to overwhelm your life, I strongly urge you to seek therapy. It is so helpful to have an objective stranger point out your behaviors to you. Sure, it can feel like a shock to your system, but I feel that we're on this planet to learn, to evolve, and to change. Working on yourself, whether it be modalities you're interested in, healing work, or other methods, can also be transformative. Your journey will be life-long but so worth it.

CLEARING ENERGY

Clearing energy is an ongoing process. Our spiritual life consists of the energy, the universal life flow, that flows in every one of us to connect us all. It is referred to by different words in other practices, such as Prana in Hinduism, Qi (or Chi) in Taoism, Reiki for Reiki practitioners, and other terms you might be familiar with in your spiritual journey. Doing regular spiritual hygiene is a good practice for Positive Pagans. Sometimes we might not be aware of how other people's energies affect us until we notice that we feel off, whether it be unusually sad or irritated, seemingly out of nowhere. It's just like dirt on your skin, except you need to clean this off internally. If you neglect to maintain your spiritual hygiene, it can affect so much: how you think and feel, how you are perceived, your surroundings, and more. It can allow fear and stress into your life, and then the spiral into darkness begins.

BOUNDARIES

To begin monitoring your energy fields, I recommend doing a check of your boundaries. Ah, that word. Most people aren't comfortable with boundaries at all and are wide open to all experiences and energies.

To begin, check how you feel around certain people. Are there some people in your life who poke and pry into your personal life, and you don't feel comfortable? Is there a friend who always talks about themselves, yet never asks about you? Do you feel irritated, but let it pass, because of your friendship? Is it a friend or relative who is gloom and doom in all their conversations, no matter if good things happen in their life or not? Do any of these ring a bell? Boundaries can be as simple as removing yourself from an uncomfortable conversation. Many people worry about being rude, but you can practice. The world will not end, and you can move onward. If the other person gets irritated, remember that they are responsible for their own reaction, and your friendship will survive. If it doesn't, then offer your friend a chance to discuss their feelings on the subject and see if you can manage a dialogue about it. If this is ongoing, take a pause and consider what joy this friendship brings you. Staying friends merely out of habit is a disservice to you both. Friendship at its best is supportive, caring, and inspirational. If it's the complete opposite end of the spectrum, then you should reconsider that relationship.

Boundaries can be verbal, physical, and metaphysical in nature. Only you can decide what you're comfortable with, so start out with some small adjustments and see how it feels. I find boundaries to be like muscles. It may hurt a bit at first, but keep using that muscle and set those boundaries. Remember that it is up to you to set the boundaries at the level that it is respected.

If setting boundaries with friends seems too difficult for you, here is another way to shift your friend's energy toward you.

Boundary Letter

Items Needed:
Protection incense (your own or purchased)
Paper
Favorite writing instrument
Florida Water

Light your incense and sit in a comfortable spot. Begin writing a letter to your friend, outlining how they make you feel when they don't respect your boundaries. Within that letter, forgive them for their actions. If forgive is too strong a word for you (note: that's a boundary), then use the term "energy adjustment" in its place. The purpose of this letter is to adjust your friend's energy toward you. When you have written to your satisfaction, take the letter and send your energy out to the recipient. When done, sprinkle Florida Water on the letter and your hands. Rub your hands together and massage your body from the top of your head down to your feet, clearing the energy. You don't have to send this letter. You can recycle it, burn it in your cauldron, or put it aside if you want to continue working on it as the need arises.

(Note: You can also clear your energy with a selenite wand or a sprig of rosemary.)

Checking your spiritual boundaries may seem a bit easier. Check your energy from the top of your head to the bottom of your feet. If you notice any part of your body feels a bit off, try some of the following to clear yourself.

Water Clearing

Another way to quickly clear your energy is to utilize Sun Water, Full Moon Water, any Sacred Water you've collected, or Florida Water. Set the intention of clearing your energy, dip your fingers in the water, and touch all your energy points from the top of your head down to your feet. Let your intuition guide you as to what needs clearing.

Nature Clearing

Go to your favorite nature spot. Find a patch of grass, take off your shoes, and root your feet firmly on the ground. Feel the energy from the top of your head going downward, past your feet and into the ground. Or hug a tree so you can feel the tree's energy, letting it move through you. If you're on a path in the forest, and you feel comfortable, look upward past the tree into the sky and reach your hands up as far as you can. Take a huge deep breath and exhale noisily. Take another one, and then another. How does that feel? Do a quick body scan and thank the nature you see before you.

Crystal Clearing

Pagans know to charge their crystals under the Full Moon to clear the energy, so find a crystal that you resonate with, and imbue it with cleansing energy. You can do this yourself via your own energy, or you can pass the crystal through your favorite incense or douse in Florida Water or whatever spiritual water you like. Use this crystal to hold when you feel tense, and also as a guide to clear your energy from the top of your head to your feet.

Symbol Clearing

Sometimes when nothing is readily available, and you're not able to access nature, water, your crystals, or anything else, you can use a symbol to provide clearing energy. You can draw it on your hand, over your heart, in the air in front of you like a protective shield, or wherever you feel guided to clear.

Consider which symbols mean the most to you, and let it guide your creation of a new symbol for your personal use. If possible, form a little ritual around its creation. Light a candle, burn some incense, meditate upon the symbol under the New Moon, and draw it when you feel you have one whose energy will clear you. My symbol incorporates a spiral, since I consider my life to be a spiral, and it has powerful energy to me. It may be simple or intricate; only you know what works for you. Keep this symbol between you and your deities so that its power is unadulterated.

Sound Clearing

There are practitioners you can visit for sound clearing, but if you need some immediate assistance, use sound to clear your energy field. It can be as easy as driving in your car with your favorite music turned up, a Tibetan singing bowl, or a strike on a stainless-steel object (my stainless-steel water bottle has been useful for this). Local church bells might help if you find the sound comforting (some don't). Chanting is also a good way to clear energy, so find some on YouTube or keep them on your playlist to use during times such as these.

Whatever you use for clearing, do it often, and if life gets busy as it often does, set a calendar reminder to do it at least every New Moon. It's good for you and your environment, so let that energy and magic flow through you as needed so you can continue being the Positive Pagan that you are!

Language Clearing

Language is powerful spellwork, and how we speak to ourselves and others has an effect. Sure, we have times when we're in a hurry and careless, but may we all strive to do better. I find so many people with verbal crutches such as "Does that make sense?" "I'm so stupid, careless, silly, greedy, etc." Insert whatever negative attribute there, and you'll see what I mean.

Flip your language around to a more positive manner and begin the habit of carefully weighing what you say. Take small steps. If you often apologize, then examine what you are apologizing for so many times. If you are habitually late, you can say you're working on a time-management problem. Don't apologize endlessly for actions you take because the apologetic words become meaningless. Do you find yourself apologizing all day long? Examine why and resolve to not say it as much. Try going for one day, then two days, and onward. See how different you feel.

Make more space for silence in your life. Set aside time daily to be still and listen to the world around you. Don't rush into filling silences with words if you are with friends or having a conversation. Find the comfortable feeling in those silences and see what happens.

One more verbal crutch I would like to make note of is: "I could kill myself" or "I just want to shoot myself in the head." Please don't say either of these. Once you have experienced life with suicide by a loved one, those words hurt. I flinch when people say either because humans actually do these things, and the wreckage left behind can be unbearable. It goes back to being in the moment, aware, and mindfully moving through your life.

Take a moment to note which verbal crutches you use, and what you can say instead. Instead of "I'm late," you can say, "Thank you for waiting" (much more positive).

A POSITIVE PAGAN YEAR

Each month, we are given the unique gift of renewing ourselves. Each Full Moon we are given a chance for reflection and release. We have the chance to flourish in our positivity, hit the reset button if we need to, and celebrate. If you follow the Wheel of the Year, add in secular holidays or your own personal observances so that each month results in many positive celebrations. Here are suggestions for each month, along with a specific Full Moon ritual. But know that the most powerful rituals and celebrations are the ones you create yourself.

January

Ah, January! The most restful time of the year, usually full of free evenings and more sleep due to winter weather (if that happens where you are). It's a great time for vision boards, getting journals started, and planning for Imbolc in February. Get hygge with it (the Danish way of bringing coziness and contentment in your life). If you are orderly, get more order in your life with new systems or methods. It's a great time to clear out the old and make way for the new. The whole vista of the year is before you! What do you want to do with your wondrous year? If you garden, gather your seed catalogs and lists of supplies. Celebrate the Wolf Moon!

Wolf Moon Ritual

Using white candles and white pine (essential oil or white pine needles) to clear and consecrate your space, do a full year divination reading, one for each month. Journal which cords you'd like to cut, and which ties from last year that you'd like to sever. Cleanse your home with Florida Water, sacred smoke, and incense. Play your favorite magical music and prepare a small feast for you and your deities. Dance under the moon (stay warm!) and rejoice in candlelight. If you are able to have a fire, do so, but if not, use a large white candle to do some candle scrying and gaze into this coming year.

February

Imbolc! Time to celebrate the halfway mark to spring. If you celebrate Imbolc, stretch your time of celebration to weeks instead of just one day. Wear red and gold all month (red is also good for Valentine's Day) and get a Brigid's Wheel to guard your house and strengthen your home's protection. Valentine's Day is not just about romantic relationships, it's about LOVE. We love many ways: friends, family, animals, nature, ourselves. Find something to love, and really lavish your attention and love on it. It could be caretaking an indoor herb plant, fostering or adopting a new pet, helping a friend who is going through hard times, comforting a lonely co-worker, or assisting an elderly neighbor. Celebrate the Snow Moon!

Snow Moon Ritual

Use red or gold candles; pour milk in your bath to honor the Goddess Brigid; write poetry or whatever your heart is moved to write, possibly a letter to your love, whether it be family, friend, or yourself; and focus on what you'd like spring to bring forth for you. If you'd like to bring love into your life, set up an altar filled with rose quartz, rose petals, magical love oil, cinnamon, sugar, and lavender or honey offerings. If you know the attributes of the person you want to bring into your life, list them on a piece of paper. Tear each individual attribute into a strip and place it in a beautiful box or jar. Make it a practice to read these attributes aloud nightly until the next Full Moon. Make some space in your closet and bedroom for the person you want to bring into your life and consecrate it. If you don't have altar space for your love offerings, then place a few of the items (rose quartz, cinnamon sticks, rose petals) in a bowl of rice and place it under your bed.

March

Spring is here! Ostara is celebrated, Spring Equinox is here, and all beginnings seem to be symbolized with eggs. Eggs are the circle of life in many cultures, so celebrate that egg mightily. The weather is warmer in most cases, so head outside if that is true for your area. Get back to nature, hug those trees, and celebrate St. Patrick's Day if you have Celtic leanings. You don't have to drink the beer, but you can make some yummy Irish treats, such as Irish soda bread.

Purchase a shamrock plant and plan a possible trip to Ireland, if that's been on your list. March is also a good reset button, because, honestly, you can reset anytime. Reset it with spring, a new season, and a time for opening up to the rest of the year. Do you feel the quickening energy, even if you don't see anything blooming just yet? If you have been hibernating in January and February, then start to blossom in March. Get some tulips to remind you of your blooming. Celebrate the Worm Moon!

Worm Moon Ritual

Use green and yellow candles, decorate eggs with natural dyes (onions for yellow, spinach for green, see what you come up with as you immerse hard-boiled eggs into these natural colors). Then ritually dispose of these magical eggshells by burning them or casting them in a flowing river away from you. Dig deep inside yourself to see what is out of balance. Dig deep with your hands into the earth and enjoy the warmer days.

April

April showers bring May flowers, so work on the water aspect of your altar. Visit lakes, streams, oceans, creeks, wells, and more. Spend some time really pondering the fluidity of water, how it changes landscapes while merely existing, and doing what it does best: flowing. Is there flow in your life? If not, what is keeping things from flowing? Examine blockages and see what you can do to remove them. April is a good time to work on abundance, especially as tax season is over. If you'd like to learn something new, April is a great month to begin as the weather warms up and life seems easier as daylight stays with us longer throughout our day. Enjoy your garden if you planted one and observe the beauty of nature around you. Celebrate the Pink Moon!

Pink Moon Ritual

Use pink and red candles, pink and red rose petals, pink Himalayan salt (or natural sea salt), a bowl of natural or filtered water, and rose quartz and floating candles. Use this moon to send love out to others. Write their names down on strips of paper and add the salt, rose petals, and rose quartz to the bowl of water. Stirring clockwise, add the names one by one to the water. Light the floating candles and let them float upon the water. Envision the candle fire neutralizing any negativity between you and those you love and use the energy from the petals and salt to send your love out to them, wherever they are.

May

Merry, merry Beltane is here! Is it always Beltane in your heart? Celebrate that, as all acts of pleasure are done in honor of the Goddess. Celebrate your goddesses, wear a flower crown often, and plan more time outdoors. Attend a festival, either Pagan or secular, and enjoy exploring. Work on your gardens, visit local landmarks, and be a tourist in your hometown. Notice all the beautiful flowers in your area and learn more about them. Do you want to learn more about herbs? Then do so online or in-person. Grab a few books for quiet evenings spent in candlelight. Celebrate the Flower Moon!

Flower Moon Ritual

Us red, orange, and yellow candles and gather bouquets of flowers, large or small. If you don't already have one, and are able to do so, get a fire pit. If you are not able to have a fire where you live, gather a few small sticks for your cauldron. Light whichever fire you can and try some fire divination. What do you see in the flames? Create your own flower crown or necklace and wear them as you gaze into the fire. Take what you see and create stories and tales from the symbols. Think of how you will blossom as the sun grows warmer and the plants burst forth with their bounty.

June

Remember that feeling of exhilaration when you got out of school? Find that feeling again, whether it be an activity, driving with the windows open and your favorite music playing, or running in your neighborhood. Explore different types of drinks as your focus is on hydration for your body. See if there are other ways you can stay hydrated: adding fruit or herbs to pitchers of ice water or your water bottle. Enjoy the beginning of summer, and let the sun warm your body (while using plenty of sunscreen). Litha is upon us, so how will you celebrate? It's the longest day of the year, so enjoy the delights of the year. Have a bonfire or organize one with friends. There is a definite sensual enjoyment to dancing around a fire, so try it if you haven't done so before. Enjoy the Strawberry Moon!

Strawberry Moon Ritual

Charge a bowl of freshly picked strawberries under the Full Moon, and eat them the next day so that you can feel the power of the moon inside you. Create a fruit punch or sangria with strawberries and do the same. Research the magical significance of strawberries and devise your own ritual with them. Add strawberry slices to wine or water for your ritual and use them in the meals you prepare during this time.

July

The peak of summer is during this month, so enjoy all the aspects that July has to offer. Make pitchers of lemonade, cool off with bountiful salads, and make popsicles. Summer is canoeing lazily, reading books in a hammock, and cooling off in a movie theater on a hot afternoon. Enjoy all the bounty of fruits and vegetables, grill out with friends, and make time for play. Play is often not part of our vocabulary as adults, so rediscover what play is to you: sports? Hopscotch? Jump rope? Dancing? Go to concerts if you can and enjoy music and art in all its beauty. Celebrate the Buck Moon!

Buck Moon Ritual

Brown candles represent the emerging antlers of the buck deer, after which this month is named. What growth is pushing through for you? Is your spirituality still a bit muddled, but a few nudges happen here and there? Clear off your altar and set it anew with a focus on your deities or your spirituality. Get a new statue or an item from nature to adorn your altar, use a fresh altar cloth, and clean and consecrate all items on your altar anew.

August

It's back to school for many, so let this month be a reset for you as well. If your family needs an overhaul on your schedule, get that organized. If you need to squeeze in a last-minute vacation before the fall, do so, and truly enjoy time spent away from the day-to-day. Look ahead to fall, planning out projects and beginning preparations for Samhain. Lughnasadh / First Harvest is celebrated (also called Lammas). I have begun a tradition of baking bread to honor the month. I set intentions in the bread and focus on what I need to accomplish by the end of the year, both personally and professionally. Celebrate the Sturgeon Moon!

Sturgeon Moon Ritual

Green and grey candles represent the sturgeon. Grab some paper and your favorite writing instrument and try some stream-of-consciousness writing. Get into a meditative state, look deeply into the candle flames, and write without stopping or censoring. Write whatever comes to mind. When you're done, look for key words or a theme. Then scrunch up your paper and burn it. Banish any negativity that arose. Note the key words in your journal.

September

Time for Mabon and the Autumn Equinox! Second harvests are celebrated, and many look forward to the beauties of fall. What have you harvested this year so far? It is a good time to regroup and celebrate how far you've come this year, and what's ahead as the year begins to wind down. Make and wear a fall flower crown or harvest crown using mini gourds and leaves. This month always feels a bit wistful as it heads toward fall and winter, so take time to acknowledge your summer memories. Celebrate the Corn Moon!

Corn Moon Ritual

Use yellow and gold candles to honor the Corn Moon. Get a small earthenware bowl of cornmeal, take it outside, raise it skyward, and offer thanks to the moon. Walk the perimeter of your home, sprinkling the cornmeal as you go. Bring the remaining cornmeal inside and leave it as an offering on your altar.

October

Blessed month of Samhain, a busy time for many of us! Rejoice in the season, honor your ancestors, and make sure to take care of yourself. Honoring ancestors can be year-round of course, but it takes on a special meaning during this month. If you have an Ancestor Vigil this month, make plans to attend. It's a powerful, emotional time. If you don't have a community event like this nearby, consider hosting your own Dumb Supper, where you dine in silence with your ancestors. It is also powerful and moving, honoring those who have gone before. Celebrate the Hunter's Moon!

Hunter's Moon Ritual

Burn orange and black candles on your ancestor altars and veneration. Now is a good time to connect with your ancestors, so light the candles, play the music of your family's ethnic background, and make offerings of food and drink that would be pleasing to them. Sit down in darkness, lit only by the candles, and talk to your ancestors. Tell them about yourself, memories of your youth, and retell family folklore. If you are unfamiliar with your family heritage, be open and receptive to hearing from your ancestors. A nugget or two of information might be revealed.

November

A time of thanks, more so than any other time. Fraught with family tension? Slow down and enjoy the gratitude sentiment of Thanksgiving. Lots of deep breaths to navigate your world if this holiday fills you with dread instead of anticipation. An exercise that I like to do at this time of year is taking stock. For all the negative things that have happened, I like to list the grateful outcomes. An example: Got fired from one job, which led to getting the job of my dreams. Relationship ended, which led to an even better one. Got really sick, which led to me discovering my true tribe. One caveat: Do this exercise only if you have some distance to see the positive outcome. Only you will know if you are ready to see the positive outcome of what's happened. This exercise helps you note how far you have come, and how you have survived 100 percent to this very moment. Celebrate the Beaver Moon!

Beaver Moon Ritual

Light yellow, red, orange, and gold candles in your ritual space. Prepare the space and take a moment to gaze into the lit candles. Place a bowl of water on your altar and hold a bowl of small glass stones in your hand. Think of things you are grateful for, and as you say each one out loud, place a stone in the water. When you are done or have used up all the stones, take the heads of the orange and yellow flowers and float them on top of the water in the bowl.

December

Yule! Winter Solstice, greenery, and multitudes of candles. Celebrate the gifts both tangible and heartfelt, and the joy of the season. It can be hard to find joy this month since everyone can seem to be in horrific moods, but I have found focusing on candles help me through those feelings of overwhelm. Nightly lighting candles, whether in a menorah, an advent wreath, or any of the beautiful holiday candles available, is a soothing ritual. Find songs to sing, create special treats, or read Winter Solstice books to soothe yourself from the outside world. Celebrate the Cold Moon!

Cold Moon Ritual

Use white and gold candles. Write down all that you have achieved in the year and note what you have not. Do you want to carry them into your new year? If yes, write these down, along with a list of your New Year's resolutions, and place the paper in a jar. Decorate the outside of the jar with glue and glitter or a collage of magazine photos that symbolize your resolutions. Place the gold candle on top of the jar and let it burn down to seal the energy of your intent.

As the circle closes on the year, and you look toward a new year, take notice of how far you have come. Create a Celebration Board, similar in concept to the Vision Board. Celebrate what you have accomplished, not just in your work, but in your life. Are you celebrating sobriety or an ordination? Have you become proficient in herbalism or a new language? Have you finished up a chapbook of poems, created beautiful quilts, or fed your family from your garden? All things to celebrate. Make it festive with a glitter frame or outline in whatever makes you feel delighted. Stars? Your favorite colors? Photos of friends? Be as creative as you'd like and use this celebration as you near the beginning of the new year. Let it be your New Year's Eve activity if you want to stay in and be cozy. Most of all, celebrate the Full Circle of YOU.

BALANCE

Balance is a word that is used often nowadays, but honestly, can we truly find balance? I feel as if balance is sometimes only momentarily felt, and I am perfectly okay with that. They are small victories in this thing we call life. It doesn't mean we shouldn't strive for balance, or that it is completely elusive. We can strive for balance in our day, in the foods we eat, in our social interactions, in our work and play, and attempt to balance our positive side with our negative.

What does balance feel like? I liken it to achieving that sense of rightness when you are balanced on a swing. When you feel balanced, you can soar ever higher, yes? If the swing is wonky, you will hit other swings or swing more side to side than way up in the sky. Balance is when the horizon is clear and even ahead of you, the feeling of a beautiful sunrise or sunset. It's achieved when you've had a glorious day filled with fulfilling activity, healthy and yummy meals, are fully hydrated, and you have had enough energy for everything, ending with drifting off to a restful sleep.

A Balancing Ritual

Items Needed:

4 Mason jars, all the same height

A tray

All 4 elements: earth, air, fire, and water

4 candles to represent the elements: each can be brown, white, red, and blue. Candleholders for each, if needed.

Journal and pen

Place the 4 Mason jars on the tray. Fill each jar with an element: dirt for earth, breathe heavily into one jar for air, symbolize fire with a lighter or matchbox, and fill the last jar with water. Use whichever symbols you like or paste pictures of each element onto each jar. Line them up in a row so you can see them clearly.

Call in your guardians and ancestors and have them join you in this ritual. Face in all four directions in the order you prefer, and note the elements of each: earth, of mountains and rock, water of oceans and lakes, etc.

Light the four candles and spend time in contemplation as you gaze into the candles.

Individually take each jar and again note all of the different aspects of the elements. For example: *Earth is home, North, dirt under my fingers in my garden, mountains, sand at the beach, the floor on which I sit.* Do that for each one.

Now close your eyes and begin to fill each jar with the aspects of the elements within you. For earth, consider all the earthy parts of you going into the jar. It can be the lethargy you are feeling, the solids of your fingernails or hair, the salt from your body. Envision it going into the jar. When the first jar is complete, do the same for the rest of the jars, one after the other. When finished, take some deep breaths.

You have emptied the elements into the jars. Now imagine replenishing yourself and filling your body with the elements of earth, air, fire, and water, in whatever forms call to you. The dirt under your hands as you plant a garden, welcome that. The cool breeze that surrounds you on a hot day, welcome that. The water of a refreshing swimming hole that only you know about, welcome that. The fire of a cozy fireplace, welcome that. When you feel replenished, hug yourself and rejoice in saying out loud, *Blessed Be!*

When you're finished, get out your journal. Describe how you felt once you were replenished. All the sensations, the thoughts you had, and how you feel now. Date this entry and return to it when you feel depleted.

Lunar Balance

Drawing down the moon can also help replenish your energy when you feel depleted. When the moon is full, head outside where you can see it clearly. Make sure you will not be disturbed, so do this in your backyard or in a safe, local nature spot. Stand under the moon, gazing at her beauty and noting the glow. When ready, hold your hands out as if you are embracing the moon. Feel the energy draw through your fingers, hands, and arms. Absorb as much energy as you feel you need and hug yourself in silent appreciation when you're done. I like to say "thank you" to the moon when completed.

Notice how you feel after communing with lunar energy. You may feel more energized at New Moons, and quiet and contemplative with the Full Moon. As it waxes and wanes, notice if it affects your balance, or if you feel more of a pull at new and Full Moons. There are several online moon apps that will help you keep track of the moon's position.

Take a month to journal your emotions on each day and notice how the moon cycles affect you. You may be drawn more to the energy of a New Moon versus a Full Moon, so adjust your spellwork and intention setting to whichever moon works best for you.

Finding yourself in sync with the moon energies is a grounding experience. You feel more connected to nature itself, and you may find yourself moving through the world in a different way.

Circle Balance

When life feels out of balance, I like to draw a huge circle and try to ascertain which parts are taking up space in my life. This is a pie chart of your life, and if balanced, should resemble a delightful pie in three even slices. If parts of your life are taking over more of the pie than others, make note of which aspect it is, and brainstorm ways you can get more in balance. If work is taking on more of your life than anything else, what can you do? Get up earlier and carve out self-care time? Delegate some of your work so that you're not working so late? Conversely, if your social life is eating into your work time, reduce your social obligations so that you're back in balance. If self-care takes a hit from work and social, then block out time for things that make you feel taken care of, whether it be scheduling a Friday night bath, a monthly pedicure or massage, or solid alone time on the weekends.

Balance of Dark and Light

Being a Positive Pagan doesn't mean that you're cheerful and peppy all the time. If you find yourself in a dark place, take note of what the darkness is about, whether it be past experiences you revisit, a relationship that isn't quite ended, or behavior that you should probably stop. Being a Pagan, there is power behind your actions, so remember that action helps. If it consists of writing down all that you need to shed and burning that paper in a cauldron, do it. It can be cathartic. If it means taking a ritual bath to get the ick of the week off you, then do so. If it means strengthening your personal shields and the protection of your home, then make it happen. Often we feel helpless because we think we can't change anything, but we do have the power, and can effect change. All it takes is that first step. If you work with deities and your ancestors, then invite them to do so. You may soon find stepping stones appearing in front of you, guiding your way.

Balance Within Yourself

How are you keeping yourself balanced? Do you find yourself swinging about dramatically like a pendulum? Are you encompassing the foundations of meditation, exercise / moment, breath-work, and eating well? You may roll your eyes at this part because we all know this, yes? Yet how many of you have these foundations firmed up? Start out slowly if all four areas (or any of them) need a boost. Meditate for five minutes a day, go for a quick walk after work, and practice four-part breathing (four-count breath in, hold for four counts, four counts as you exhale, hold for four counts). Skip fast food entirely for a week and take note of how you feel.

Know yourself and what feeds you to keep yourself in that state of balance. What feeds you emotionally, spiritually, and physically? Do you have a spiritual practice in place? Is it satisfying? Do you have a deity, deities, or a Higher Power that you work with on a regular basis, or just as needed? Do you take part in rituals or community rituals? Do you have a community that feels supportive, or do you prefer being a solitary practitioner? Do you communicate regularly with your ancestors? Do you honor them, either regularly or at Samhain? Is your ancestor dusty or tucked away somewhere? Or have you lost track of it?

There are no absolute answers, as only you know what's needed. As you read through the questions, did you feel a tug from any of them?

Reflect in your journal the following: Write down the questions that resonated for you, the answers you want to give to those questions, along with a plan of action, if needed.

REMOVE BLOCKS

Along with the foundations, look next at your goals and projects. Are there ones you have been putting off for a while? Do you feel blocked or thwarted?

The quickest way to remove blockages is a salt bath.

Unblocking Salt Soaking Bath

Items Needed:

Full cup of sea salt

Orange candles (for road opening) or blue candles (for creativity block)

Draw a bath and dissolve the sea salt within the water. Light your candles and soak in the water for at least 30 minutes. Keep your water bottle nearby so that you can stay hydrated while soaking. Call on your deity, deities, or Higher Power. Ask for their help and envision a wide-open road while you soak.

Balancing yourself can also involve stretching yourself, whether it be with a new skill, new habit, adding to your knowledge, or stretching your patience. Find time each week to stretch yourself.

Get out your journal. List five ways in which you can stretch yourself in the coming weeks. Maybe you will cook dinner at home more often, add a new ritual to your celebrations, or explore a new skill. List activities that you have been wanting to explore but haven't made time to before now. Resolve to try at least one in the coming weeks.

KNOWING THYSELF

Sometimes we are so busy focusing outwardly that we neglect to get to know our favorite person of all: ourselves. Do you know yourself very well? Do you know the basics, such as all your favorites? What scares you? What challenges you? What inspires you? If you find yourself not knowing much about your own self, I urge you to get to really know yourself.

You may have gotten the impression that you're quiet and boring, without much to offer. Maybe you tried to do different things, and they didn't turn out well, so you didn't try again. Possibly you keep to yourself and a strict routine, with no outside influences. Whoever you are, I assure you that you're fascinating. There is only one you, so begin with that. No one else has lived your life, and no one has had your experiences. Maybe you had talents you explored at one time, or hobbies you used to enjoy. Revisit those. Interview yourself and ask the sort of questions you'd ask someone you just met. What would you like to know about someone? Ask those questions of yourself.

Do you have a person in your life that helps you feel balanced? That person can help with accountability as you strive for balance. If you start an exercise program, plan to read a book a week, or work on a skill, a friend can encourage, support, and remind you. It's also a great way to keep in touch, especially if that friend is not nearby. And you can certainly be accountability partners for each other! Sounds much better than fending for yourself, right?

Balance can also be putting one foot in front of the other. As simple as that. Keep moving forward, and balance will be regained. Your actions will affect what is going on with your life, so if there is a lack, see what you can do to fill that need. Rituals and spellwork are actions. Accessing the power of the new and Full Moons is an action. And working with your guardians and ancestors is an action. Action ultimately helps you feel better, and in turn makes you want more of that feeling. The journey to find that balance may seem never-ending, but along the way, you can discover things about yourself that will delight you, make you think, and inspire change.

Journal Prompt

What is out of balance for you at the moment?

In reading this chapter, what ideas will you implement to help restore balance?

What causes the imbalance for you? Can you identify them? If not, take some time to ponder habits or routines that you can tweak to bring more balance to that imbalance. If yes, what steps can you take to remove the cause of imbalance?

CHAPTER 10

Onward and Upward

The phrase "Onward and Upward!" has helped to encourage me throughout my life. In turn, I have encouraged others with this phrase when troublesome times have occurred. It is an uplifting phrase that also signifies a boundary, moving onward from where you've been, and upward, signifying a positive direction. It is my motto and touchstone when I have moved through some challenges, and my intention for people when they need a boost.

What does it mean, exactly? Onward is moving forward, and that momentum will propel you through life, moving you through your life's journey. Stories keep our world revolving, so if you can find parts of your story that inspire others, then please share them so they can be inspired. Our stories are our connection in this world! There is much we can learn from each other.

People's choices and triumphs help inspire other people, because, let's face it, we can all feel utterly alone at points in our life. Hearing or reading about other's challenges can inspire us to keep one foot in front of the other, try different methods, envision a different outlook, and give us hope. Hope is a hard thing to find in this crazy world. We can't go backward and change anything, but we can move onward and make things better. Onward feels like progress and movement. It feels positive and energizing. It feels hopeful and powerful.

Blessed Be to you as you go throughout your days as you journey in your life. Share your tips on how you learned and survived and help the person behind you (metaphorically and literally) move forward as well. Onward is the exhilaration of leaving behind what no longer serves, and the weight of what held you back diminishing or disappearing. Onward is moving somewhere else or starting a new job. Onward is a new relationship that finally works after all the other ones didn't. Onward is knowing your children are lovely human beings. Onward is losing that weight you wanted to or quitting smoking. Onward is anything that makes you happy you are alive. Onward is being happy to wake up to a new day. Onward is hope, love, peace, and feeling centered and grounded.

Upward is a trajectory. Upward into the beautiful blue sky, and upward to your dreams. No longer pie in the sky, as the saying goes, but your dreams becoming reality. Upward is also achieving that which you seek, whether it be visible or personal satisfaction. Upward is movement, again leaving behind that which no longer serves us. Do you feel the beauty of letting go of what held you back? Do you feel the wind rush past you as you race toward your goal? Do you feel that inner spark of having your life back on track when it's been so completely derailed? Upward is taking flight, moving up ladders, and climbing mountains. Upward is moving to the top floor, the rooftop view, the apex of your dreams. Upward is reaching up right now, with both hands in the air, standing on tiptoe, as high as you can reach. Feel the stretch and the joy. Upward is a paper airplane, filled with written words of your dreams, taking flight on a clear, sunny day. Upward is that fist pump when you finally mastered that thing you thought you never would.

Onward and Upward with your spiritual practice as well. This book is meant to enhance your spiritual practices, whatever tradition you follow. It is my hope they give you clarity and a spark to deepen your practice. If your spiritual practices have fallen by the wayside, I hope you find the joy in rediscovering them.

Being a Positive Pagan is not done in a vacuum. Sure, you can feel like a Positive Pagan all by yourself in the middle of nowhere, with few people to talk to and affect your positivity. Yet your actions do send out an energy into the world similar to a ripple in a lake. Let it ripple out and affect those around you. If you and I do it, it affects two groups of people in our midst. If you and I and thousands of fellow people do this, imagine the effect on the planet. Being a Positive Pagan is also a mindset. Once you are in this mindset, life will feel as if it's flowing through you, and moving you forward. When you feel that rush of positive energy, you will want more of it.

As you journey Onward and Upward, here are a few more tenets of Positive Paganism to keep that positivity going.

ZERO EXPECTATIONS

This is one of my constant reminders, and I cannot emphasize this enough. Manage your expectations because dissonance happens when we try to control outcomes. You can and should have a vision of what you would like to have happen, but be open to possibility. If you have zero expectations, it frees you from disappointment and leaves you open to discover other delightful avenues and possibilities. If you start at zero, you can only go up from there, right? Keep that in mind. Have a vision but let go of the control of it.

GUARD YOUR ENERGY

I cannot stress this one strongly enough. Please guard your energy. Guard it fiercely when needed. It is setting a boundary to be sure. Along with taking care of yourself, guarding your energy is an important tenet. Consider it the most valuable part of you because your energy is your life flow. Say no to people and events that drain you and instead turn to that which nourishes you. Don't feel obligated to attend something if it makes you feel horrible. Don't tolerate a friendship that is ultimately draining. Consider joining another group if the one you are in has gone down a path you are not comfortable with. Or start your own group. Guilt is often mentioned as a reason to keep doing things which no longer serve us, but guilt is a wasted emotion. If you regret certain actions, that is a different story. Regret and guilt are two different things, and guilt is often a feeling that we use to make ourselves feel bad about our choices. If you view it as a choice you made with all the information you had available at the time, then that shifts the energy to something that is regrettable, but not something you should spend repetitive energy over. You cannot go backward and change what happened, but you can make a choice to change moving forward.

As time moves onward, our needs and feelings change. Please honor them and be unafraid to move in new directions. Guarding your energy is not a selfish act; it is self-preservation, and the results are so worthwhile: a happier, more focused, and centered YOU.

MANIFESTING

Move the energy toward what you want. If you are not sure what you want, go back and work on that first. Maybe start out small with some basics: a different job, travel, a new place to live. Apply the zero expectations here as well, because you don't know how it will show up. One of my favorite manifestation stories is about a woman who wanted to go on a cruise. She had it on her vision board and tried to save, but the goal seemed impossibly far away. She kept envisioning it though and remained positive. One day, a good friend called and said she had won a cruise via a radio contest. Would she go with her? Voilà! The cruise manifested, but not in the way she assumed it would. She was open to possibility, stayed positive, and it happened for her.

Love Bowl Ritual

A love bowl is a magical way to bring love into your life. Note that it is for love, not a specific person. It is better energetically to manifest love in your life, rather than a specific person, even if you have your eye on someone special. Why? Because we all have our own free will and magic itself will not bring that person to you. Better to let go of expectations (sound familiar?) and work toward manifesting more love in your life.

> Items Needed:
> *Ceramic bowl*
> *Natural brown rice*
> *Crystals associated with love*

First, find a beautiful ceramic bowl. Thrift shops are wonderful and inexpensive places to find bowls such as these. Fill the bowl halfway with some natural brown rice. Next, choose crystals associated with love: rose quartz, amber, garnet, and moonstone are a few good choices. Place the bowl under your bed and let it do its work. Send some love energy toward it. Check on it periodically for dust bunnies and to reinforce the love intentions. Be open to possibility and note the love that comes into your life with this working.

NETWORKING

That doesn't sound too magical, does it? Yet, for lack of a better term, networking works to bring people into your life. Being open to meeting people can open your network to other people who may end up being good friends, supporters, and confidants. Think of it like a ripple and throw a stone into your community and see what happens. Be open to possibility and see who you meet, either online or in person. Trust your intuition to find members of your vibe tribe or however you want to refer to your community. I've always enjoyed the phrase, "Your vibe attracts your tribe," so if your vibe is positive, filled with what makes you uniquely you, then you will attract similar people. Community can be wonderful, helping you through challenging times and helping ease loneliness. It is up to you for how much or how little community you want. Introverts need to guard against being too isolated, extroverts need to be discerning about their relationships (energy vampires and toxic relationships are just two that come to mind), and ambiverts need to find a balance between both introversion and extroversion because too much of one can be draining. Enjoy building your network because the end result can be a vibrant and nourishing tribe that will sustain and inspire you.

MANTRAS/POSITIVE SAYINGS

Mantras and positive sayings can merely seem like a pithy reminder or quote, and you can move through your life without paying them much attention. However, if you view them as signposts or reminders in life, they may resonate with you differently. If one crosses your social media feed, be open to receiving their messages and see if you can apply them to your situation. Quotes can give you perspective and allow you to view a situation differently. It can also point you in a different thought pattern, which may help if you are feeling stuck or uninspired. Then there are those quotes that come at just the right time, helping you with something that is bothering you at that time.

How do you turn a quote into something magical? If you find one that resonates with you, print it out or use calligraphy to create a focal point for your altar. Place it in a frame of your choice and place a white or gold candle in a candleholder in front of it. You can sprinkle some glitter on the words or place some faux gems on the picture frame. Be creative as you'd like in the presentation. For a period of time (start with a week and go from there), light the candle and spend some time really contemplating the words. See if you can come up with your own version, make up a song about it, or write a poem. Let those words resonate within you and see how you feel. When you feel complete, remove the quote and place it in a special box or your Book of Shadows. Repeat this when you see other quotes that resonate.

ROLE MODELS

It helps to have certain role models, whether literary or in real life. Growing up, books such as *Jane Eyre* and *A Tree Grows in Brooklyn* had a special place in my heart because those characters survived adversity with tenacity, determination, and a feisty spirit. They were role models for me when none were around at the time. The lessons of opportunity through adversity in those fictional worlds provided a foundation for me, and I applied those lessons to my life.

In the present day, I admire those who live truly and authentically as themselves, because their energy literally shines out of them. I may not know them personally, but they inspire me through their actions and beliefs. Look around your world and see who inspires you: it could be a community leader, a singer, a writer, or an artist.

Get out your journal. Write down who inspires you, and what you would like to do with that inspiration.

BE CURIOUS

If you are not curious about this amazing world, then you are missing out on a cornucopia of possibility! Especially nowadays with the internet and Google (I come from a time of library card catalogs), you can find out all sorts of things online and learn from the comfort of your home. Go out and explore where you live. So many times I've met people who have lived in one area their whole lives, seemingly unaware of something wonderful nearby, such as a historical monument or museum. Learn a new skill and expand your horizons. We are never too old to learn, so always add to your knowledge base when you can.

REMEMBER, DO THE WORK

Being a Positive Pagan is all about energy and intent. If you remain stagnant and don't move energy, how do you expect things to happen? Are you waiting for something to magically appear? Without moving energy and having intent, you will remain in the same space. Life is a flow of energy, waiting for you to dive in and explore. One caveat: be patient. If things don't happen right away, don't give up. Sure, it can be frustrating, but results take time. The more you practice manifesting, the easier it will be. Sometimes it may happen a bit more quickly than you expect, but not instantly. That's when you can tap into the power of the lunar cycles because they remind you of the flow of nature and provide guideposts for your workings. Look at time as a spectrum and see how far you've come! Use that energy and excitement to propel yourself forward.

BE POSITIVE

You may have noticed that this is the theme of the book. What you are attracts more of the same. So if you are sitting in pockets of doom and gloom, wouldn't it stand to reason that life would not be that stellar? Changing up your life to be more positive does require intention, energy, work, and a constant series of choices. Your life won't change if you don't put in effort, but the key is to direct that effort.

It takes practice, and there are days where it won't seem worth the effort. Keep trying though because little actions can add up to major changes. Have you ever looked back on a time period and felt like nothing happened, but when you sit and really think about it, you realize lots of things actually did happen? It's like that. Hang in there, my friend. Focus on the next five minutes of your life to get you through the rough parts and try again. The effort and results are so worth it.

THE BENEFITS OF BEING A POSITIVE PAGAN

Like a tool you may not need all the time, but with the assurance of knowing it's always there, being a Positive Pagan is within your being, full of sustenance. Use it when you can help others, or if you need an antidote to the world around us.

There are many benefits to being a Positive Pagan:

- A general sense of well-being
- Attract other like-minded people
- Expanding your friendship circle
- Being of service to your community
- More opportunities presenting themselves
- Your life will flow more steadily
- Your magical possibilities will expand
- Your (emotional, physical, spiritual) health will improve
- Life will seem full of possibilities
- Your relationship with yourself will improve

Time for reflection. Get out your journal and answer these questions: What do you think are the benefits of being a Positive Pagan? What changes have you noticed in your life as you embarked on this journey? What is your favorite part of being a Positive Pagan?

POSITIVE PAGAN MANIFESTO

Positive Paganism can be considered a movement. A movement away from the doom and gloom, the complaining and the lethargy that can sometimes happen in the Pagan community. Being positive can and has been viewed suspiciously in our community, and it's understandable. This may seem too naive or simple to navigate this increasingly complex world of ours. I disagree. Positivity is an energy that can be used to motivate and make things happen. It can be a boost to your spiritual practice, help navigate relationships and decisions, and provide a general sense of ease that is often not talked about in magical circles. People can be as fearful of the light as they can be the dark. Both places are nothing to fear if you are making informed choices and intentions. We need both light and dark to function in this world, so with a healthy respect for both, make choices and move Onward and Upward.

As you improve your outlook, note the outward ripple effect from your thoughts, actions, and words. What you do affects your immediate circle, your family, and your community.

Positive Pagans are much needed in this world because they can light the way when the world gets troubled and dark. By choosing positivity and action, we can and do make a difference.

Journal Prompt

We are at the end of our journey together in this book! As you look back over your experience reading the different ideas and rituals, what resonated for you? Which concepts do you think you will implement in your life? What did you learn about yourself in this journey?

RESOURCES

Alden, Temperance. *Year of the Witch: Connecting with Nature's Seasons through Intuitive Magick.* Newburyport, MA: Weiser Books, 2020.

Auryn, Mat. *Psychic Witch: A Metaphysical Guide to Meditation, Magick & Manifestation.* Woodbury, MN: Llewellyn Publications, 2020.

Basile, Lisa Marie. *Light Magic for Dark Times.* Beverly, MA: Fair Winds Press, 2018.

Chubb, Tanaaz. *The Power of Positive Energy.* Avon, MA: Adams Media, 2017.

Crosson, Monica. *Wild Magical Soul.* Woodbury, MN: Llewellyn Publications, 2020.

Digitalis, Raven. *The Everyday Empath: Achieve Energetic Balance In Your Life.* Woodbury. MN: Llewellyn Publications, 2019.

Forest, Danu. *Wild Magic: Celtic Folk Traditions for the Solitary Practitioner.* Woodbury, MN: Llewellyn Publications, 2020.

Lewis, Trevor. *Thriving as an Empath: Empowering Your Highly Sensitive Self.* Asheville, NC: CreateSpace Independent Publishing, 2016.

Roth, Harold. *The Witching Herbs: 13 Essential Plants and Herbs for Your Magical Garden.* Newburyport, MA: Weiser Books, 2017.

Sincero, Jen. *You Are a Badass: How to Stop Doubting Your Greatness and Start Living An Awesome Life.* Philadelphia, PA: Running Press, 2013.

Weinstein, Marion. *Personal Magic: A Modern-Day Book of Shadows for Positive Witches.* Newburyport, MA: Weiser Books, 2021.

Wigington, Patti. *The Good Witch's Daily Spellbook.* New York, NY: Fall River Press, 2016.

To Write to the Author

If you wish to contact the author or would like more information about this book, please write to the author in care of Llewellyn Worldwide Ltd. and we will forward your request. Both the author and the publisher appreciate hearing from you and learning of your enjoyment of this book and how it has helped you. Llewellyn Worldwide Ltd. cannot guarantee that every letter written to the author can be answered, but all will be forwarded. Please write to:

Lisa Wagoner
℅ Llewellyn Worldwide
2143 Wooddale Drive
Woodbury, MN 55125-2989

Please enclose a self-addressed stamped envelope for reply,
or $1.00 to cover costs. If outside the U.S.A., enclose
an international postal reply coupon.

Many of Llewellyn's authors have websites with additional information and resources. For more information, please visit our website at http://www.llewellyn.com.